A SINGULAR SPY

A SINGULAR SPY

The Untold Story of Coomar Narain

Kallol Bhattacherjee

BLOOMSBURY
NEW DELHI • LONDON • OXFORD • NEW YORK • SYDNEY

BLOOMSBURY INDIA
Bloomsbury Publishing India Pvt. Ltd
Second Floor, LSC Building No. 4, DDA Complex, Pocket C – 6 & 7,
Vasant Kunj, New Delhi 110070

BLOOMSBURY, BLOOMSBURY INDIA and the Diana logo
are trademarks of Bloomsbury Publishing Plc

First published in India 2024
This edition published 2024

ISBN: PB: 978-93-54359-32-3; e-ISBN: 978-93-54359-36-1
2 4 6 8 10 9 7 5 3 1

For sale in the Indian subcontinent only

Typeset in Fournier MT Std by Manipal Technologies Limited
Printed and bound in India by Thomson Press India Ltd

MIX
Paper | Supporting responsible forestry
FSC® C010615

To find out more about our authors and books, visit www.bloomsbury.com and sign up for our newsletters

For Keya Bhattacharya Korantak and
Shripad Korantak

Contents

Prologue

Frenzy has an old relationship with India. Once in a while, the country goes through bouts where that overwhelming force envelops it. During those moments, frenzy overpowers all else and envelopes the country's citizens. By the late 1970s, religiosity had cast a wide net across the country. Television had arrived, and Indians wanted to see their beliefs on the screen. One such frenzy gripped the country in the summer of 1981 when a total solar eclipse found mention in the media. It was difficult not to remain unaffected by the public madness that ensued after the news of the upcoming celestial event.

New Delhi was vastly different in the early 1980s. Buses were the primary mode of transportation for the masses. Tall trees lined the broad roads. The aroma of hot spices wafting from restaurants in Connaught Place lingered in the air as exhaust fans were not as effective as they would later become. Photo studios were bustling with families and couples visiting for photo sessions, and the roads were ruled by Ambassadors and Fiats, with the rare Mercedes. Black and white photographs were still the norm, though colour film was the real craze. People would wait outside Xerox shops to get photocopies of documents, and cursive handwriting with good grammar was still a way of life. Owning a house was considered a sign of personal success.

In such a Delhi existed Geeta Farms in the Mehrauli suburbs of the city. Very few remember Geeta Farms these days. But back in 1981, it throbbed with life and flowers.

Big mango and amaltas trees kept the farm cool in the peak of summer. Cows, horses, dogs, cats and birds gave the farm its neighbourhood fame. The animals were the chosen companions of the homeowner's wife – Geetanjali. Everyone knew the middle-aged couple who owned the farm, the Narains, were in love. The homeowner would drive in his red Ambassador car every day for lunch, and the two appeared happy. The farmhouse bore the impression of the affection of Geetanjali. But destiny had other plans for the people who lived on this fertile piece of land, which had been witness to many conquests and wars in Delhi.

The commotion surrounding the solar eclipse seemed to overshadow the Narains. To a non-believer, an eclipse is simply a short-lived event when the moon briefly obscures the sun. However, for a believer, it holds a significant amount of esoteric meaning. People all over India were preparing for the event. Some had booked railway tickets to go to Kurukshetra and Prayag for a holy dip, while others, who were more scientifically oriented, had purchased dark film to watch the rare event with a camera or paper frame. However, Narain was a different man. He had acquired wealth, but he also had acquired a great fear of losing it all.

He believed in forces beyond the visual range of living beings. A little girl who was a witness to the Narain household of that time remembers a great deal of unhappiness breaking out in the house around then. Perhaps the sun and the moon had nothing to do with what was happening in the house. Perhaps it was preordained, or perhaps this is how the story of the Narains had to end.

They had lived a life of comfort and opulence and had all the trappings of success, like expensive paintings, porcelain, horses and frequently changed vehicles. But Narain, alias

Narayan, had grown progressively restless. He had begun to suspect everything and everyone as if he saw shadows chasing him all the time.

Despite the sense of doom the couple had acquired after reading the newspapers, the sun did finally come out of the eclipse after two minutes and everyone at home heaved a sigh of relief. Temple bells rang, conch shells were blown all over the country and cymbals crashed to ward off the evil spirits that might have found an invitation with the early morning eclipse.

Something began to change around that time on Geeta Farms. Geetanjali, who was known as 'Kali Mem' by the neighbourhood, began to develop a dark mood. She continuously complained of a headache and other physical problems. Her visits to the beauty parlour in Defence Colony began to dwindle. She began to wear her hair long and tied it in a big knot with a rubber band.

Her husband, who had made a fortune as a discreet business lobbyist, was increasingly scared of her mood swings, but he kept quiet. Geeta increasingly became intolerant of mistakes by her staff. Minor mistakes would often draw extreme ire, and she would lash out at her trusted aides who had served under her for years. Geeta would vent out whenever she found an occasion but would then be gripped by a crushing sense of regret and guilt. Did the eclipse bring out a memory of her secret past? Was there something that she was reminded of by the shake-up of the last few days?

The reputation of the farmhouse changed overnight.

Servants in the neighbourhood began to gossip about a mean landlady. The unpleasant news travelled back to Geeta, making her feel like the world was conspiring against her. Nothing could lift her spirits. Then, one day, she heard water flowing in the kitchen as two youngsters laughed in the background, which irritated her. After a while, she went to the kitchen to check and found her two young domestic assistants giggling over an unknown matter as they sprayed water on each other. Something ruptured inside her, and Geeta grabbed a saucer and threw it like a frisbee at the face of Radhika, one of the two young girls. As blood gushed out of Radhika's nose, Geeta came to her senses. She suddenly was her old self and screamed at the horror that she had inflicted on the young girl. She pressed the young girl's nose and began nursing her.

For days, she wept and nursed the child that she had hurt. Everyone at home was relieved that Geeta had returned to normal, but it was uncertain if this change would last. Nevertheless, it took the sight of blood for Mrs Narain to come back to her senses, even if only briefly.

The child was hurt and determined to run away from the tyrant Geeta. One day, in that injured condition, she walked out of the farmhouse. Geeta frantically looked around for Radhika but did not find her. Around midday, the police brought the child back. They had found her wandering nearby in a disoriented manner and had somehow got the address correct. They inquired Geetanjali about the still-fresh injury on the child's face and were about to force her to confess when the workers rushed out to open the gate for the red car. Narain walked in and saved his wife. In the process, he also introduced himself to the police.

This was the second time that Narain had come face-to-face with the police in his life, and his displeasure was evident. The first time was because of a run-in in the 1960s, which had caused some harm to the family's reputation. On both occasions, the damage was not to the health and well-being of the Narains but to the reputation that the two had built, bit by bit. Both Narain and Geetanjali had come to Delhi alone without any support and had built a life for themselves. It seemed the world conspired against their happiness. They were successful, but perhaps the world did not like success. Bad things happened to them whenever they were happy. The scandal of 1981 was no different. Narain was a business lobbyist, and his profession required him to have a clean reputation. One whiff of scandal and his clients and his employers could reconsider using his talents. He became careful and even more suspicious of his surroundings. Secrets – professional and personal – had to be guarded carefully if the world of the Narains had to continue undisturbed. It was only a matter of time before Narain would be subject to a frenzy of a different kind.

1

The Battlefield

India saw a major shift towards democratic access to food in 1947. For decades, Indian farmers had no control over the supply chain of their crops in the market. Despite growing bumper crops, many Indians remained hungry due to this lack of control. This problem persisted monsoon after monsoon, year after year. The famine of 1943 reminded people that though India was blessed with mighty rivers and fertile plains, they had no control over the produce.

The daily food cycle brought India closer to independence. It gave new meaning to the food market, cooking and a plate of rice and roti. However, the most important message was conveyed by the tiny bit of salt that every Indian put on their plate. For decades, Indians had paid a high price for salt – the tastemaker of the poor. The salt tax became a call for rebellion, but even the powerful Dandi march by Mahatma Gandhi could not eradicate the problem. The price of salt remained high because it was taxed unethically and linked to avarice.

It was clear that salt would be the first item to be dealt with in independent India. During the monsoon of 1946, the interim government in Delhi, which was in power until the eve of India's independence, took action to break the salt jinx. The duty on salt was one and a half rupees, but the price of a maund of salt was still Rs 5.[1] This inflated price was blamed on the inclusion of middlemen's fees. Proponents of the tax argued that the tax on salt had decreased significantly since Mahatma Gandhi's iconic march and that the government would lose valuable revenue by removing it. However, the opponents pointed out that the tax carried a sense of humiliation and removing it was a necessary political action.

The interim government abolished the tax[2] on salt by September 1946, making it more affordable for the masses. However, their main concern was to eliminate the middleman from the salt trade as the latter refused to go away, like a bad fungal infection. Although the elimination of the tax benefitted the common people, it was unlikely that it would benefit the Indian middlemen as they, with their vast information network across the commodities market and government, refused to relent. The Indian middlemen's world began to change with the arrival of telegraphic communication and news wire services like Reuters. These changes ensured that the Indian middlemen, who were known for their network in the commodities trade, were well-versed in global trade trends.[3] The middlemen were aware that the colonial masters were making more profit. Therefore, they had control over the supply side and would hold on to the produce until the European side paid the necessary amount. Being an Indian middleman was not an easy job and required continuous flexibility to stay ahead of changes in technology, news and social networks.

In 1911, the capital of India was moved from Calcutta to New Delhi. During the same year, a newspaper editorial stated, '...while the European merchant and the ryot do not now derive the profit they used to from their dealing, the Indian *middleman* makes a very fat thing out of it which would be well enough if he were a desirable member of the community. This he, unfortunately, is not, for besides being a gambler, he is a usurer of the worst sort, and any wealth he may acquire is either hoarded up in coin and jewellery instead of being used in the encouragement of the manufacturing resources of the country, or it becomes a means by which he acquires the lands of the cultivating classes and converts them from the position they have held as small land-owning farmers to that of hired labourers with no stake in the country...If ever we have a war in the land again and India becomes a cockpit for contending armies these bunnias' hoards will provide loot the like of which could not be found anywhere else in the world – Railways and Shipping'.[4] In 1911, as the world hurtled towards the First World War, the colonial empire was proud of its achievements in India – cross-country railways and shipping that connected the country with the rest of the maritime world were just two of the major achievements of that time. The predominant feeling among the people was that the worst of humankind among Indians, the middlemen, would have sold the best Indian items to the invaders if they had a chance. The middlemen, therefore, were the least honourable members of colonial society.

The middleman thrived on information about governance, and he neutralised or pre-empted every decision that was planned for him. After the colonial master was driven away, the common people of India were finally close to experiencing the fruits of independence. However, there still stood the last vestige of the old system – the middleman. This role did not disappear with the change in government. Despite efforts by the new nationalist power elite to eliminate the middleman, it became clear that there was a continuity between the colonial empire and free India that would persist, just like the famed Indian bureaucracy.

Throughout the period New Delhi, the imperial capital of India, took to grow, the middlemen remained the despised and marginalised figures. But in the end, they remained undefeated and transitioned into the new system of power in Nehruvian India. They shifted their focus from trading in agricultural commodities to machinery and hardware, and private entrepreneurs came to depend on their reach within the government, which was working to create the industrial backbone of India.

In the 1940s and 1950s, Delhi was where the new India was dreamt up and planned. The maps of two new nation-states – India and Pakistan – were drawn here. Crucial negotiations for the new republic's birth were conducted in the same city and independence was declared in the central hall of Parliament located in the capital. Yet the dark story is that hundreds of thousands of displaced people from Punjab came to the city, often losing family members in communal killings on the way. Life has its impatient cry to live, which often overpowers grief, and the grief over the Partition and the accompanying communal carnage was similarly overshadowed by the story of the success of the survivors who flourished in Delhi. Then, the city had its internal killings that continued for days and as the violence subsided, a war with Pakistan broke out over Kashmir, which kept bitter feelings alive and ultimately led to the assassination of Mahatma Gandhi – right in the middle of the new capital. At the time of Coomar Narain's arrival in Delhi, the biggest case that unveiled the capital's darker side was seen in the trial of Nathuram Godse, Madanlal Pahwa and others for the assassination of the 'Father of the Nation'.

Coomar Narain, of course, was drawn by the world of possibility that Delhi represented in the new republic. But the city was far from giving up its dark reputation shaped over centuries of power struggle and blood lust that often found expression in crime pages of newspapers.

Independence marked the beginning of a new India, but the story of Delhi was an ongoing saga, and it was to continue through iron and steel and sometimes with a bit of poison that destroyed men and women from the inside and weakened their society.

During the early decades after India's independence, Delhi was a city of hope and opportunity that attracted talented professionals from all over the country. The Nehru government recruited experts in various fields, including scientists, economists, teachers, engineers and doctors, to build a new India. Some came to pursue their artistic interests, while others aimed to accumulate wealth. However, amid the city's bright aspirations, there were also some dark secrets that occasionally intersected with the lives of the visitors. It was also the time when farmhouses became a symbol of status and fashion when the capital attracted a large number of new-generation political representatives from various corners of the country – many from rural India.

During the 1950s, when Prime Minister Nehru's son-in-law Feroze Gandhi bought one such early farm in Mehrauli, it triggered a race. Owning a farmhouse became a symbol of power and status, with people in New Delhi using the phrase 'Going to my farm during the weekend' to showcase their wealth. At that time, New Delhi was a green and lush city, but it was small and ended with a cluster of villages in and around Mehrauli. Many ambitious people from across the country flocked to the bustling capital, which had become India's most important political city. Politicians, princes and insecure aristocrats all vied for space here. However, behind the perfumed evenings of the elite and their Dimple scotch whisky sessions, there was a darker side to the city. Delhi had a reputation for being a hotbed of crime and passion, which would occasionally erupt in the form of political murder, espionage or financial scandal. What sustained that dark underbelly of Delhi's crime and passion was not understood back then; it was clear that Delhi was a city at crossroads, and it did not have control over its space. During the Nehruvian era, New Delhi was home to government officials who worked in the imperial-era offices and then withdrew into their quarters, where the dark, beastly tales of the city often unfolded. Sometimes, they unfolded amid the elite of the city. Such crimes became more frequent as the Nehru era began to mature and the spirit of the freedom movement began to ebb away. Although the leaders of the Nehru era, including Prime Minister Nehru himself, had impeccable records of probity supported by personal sacrifices they had made in the preceding decades, independence freed the bureaucracy from the fear of retribution by colonial-era administrators, and an air of permissiveness grew. This permissiveness found expression through the hidden corners of Delhi that were not often highlighted. In public, the government of Jawaharlal Nehru dealt with the pressing challenges before the country, but in the corridors of power, tales of financial mismanagement and corruption at the bureaucratic level abounded.

In 1952, India held its first democratic election under the new constitution. A year later, on the eve of Independence Day, *The Times of India* reported the scandal on its pages. The spirit of the freedom struggle was strong in India, and such stories sent expected shockwaves across the system. However, it was also understood that the top leadership of the country was not personally linked to the problem. As a result, the issue was dealt with as an aberration and not the norm. Nevertheless, these aberrations shaped the underbelly of the city, giving space for the middleman culture to flourish.

One of the first financial scandals recorded by the Indian media during the months running up to independence brought to light the extent of bureaucratic involvement and the difficulties in controlling officials who were inclined to take advantage of their powerful positions.[5] According to reports, the Joint Secretary in the Ministry of Agriculture, S.Y. Krishnaswamy, had colluded with R.M. Nanavati of Nanavati and Co. to supply Russian fertiliser at a higher price than the market rate. This case came to be known as the 'fertiliser scandal' and dated back to 1946, during the time of the interim government.

The problem's severity can be guessed from the fact that it had roots in the winter of 1946 when India was taking baby steps towards an independent future. However, that was just the beginning. Over the next few years, a series of events took place that reinforced the persistent image of Delhi as an amoral capital city that relentlessly pursues power and pelf, regardless of the cost involved.

Crime and deviance in Delhi have a long history, and over time, they became linked with the city's political nature. As a result, the authorities often bracketed political rebels and pathological criminals together. At times, crime in Delhi was linked with economic factors, such as agricultural distress in the plains surrounding the city. There were also political factors that posed an unpredictable challenge for law enforcement authorities. During the Round Table Conference-related negotiations between Mahatma Gandhi and the British government in 1932, the primary task of the police administration in Delhi province was to ensure 'security arrangements for the protection of H. E. the Viceroy, high officials, and Europeans generally'.[6] Next on the list of security priorities were top-ranking VIPs, 'the Assembly and the Council of State sessions, conferences and visits of Provincial Governors and Ruling Chiefs, fairs and processions'.[7] Besides ensuring the safety of the foreign ruling class and their Indian partners, the police were concerned about the revolutionary activities that aimed to overthrow the colonial ruling elite protected by the police. So, the police administration spent a great deal of energy scrutinising literature, pamphlets and forbidden books. The press branch of the police administration in Delhi province carried out this task. 'Revolutionaries' and their visits to the city were kept under tight watch. The responsibility of policing was enough to overwhelm a city police team anywhere in India. Such a pattern of policing openly prioritised the safety of a handful of people over the vast majority, and this problem deepened in the coming years. A section of the city had to live in a cocoon so that they never encountered the beastly conditions of their less fortunate urban co-dwellers.

After Independence, the arrangement in New Delhi changed slightly, but the separation between the ruling elite and the rest of the city remained. New entrants like Chittoor Venkat Narain would have to stand among the subjects as foreign dignitaries from non-western capitals like Moscow, Beijing and Tokyo visited India for the first time. The power elite and subjects had their respective spaces in the capital – New Delhi for the power elite and their allies and the underbelly, the alleys and far-flung parts of the city for the rest. However, clashes and negotiations between the two sections of Delhi society were a continuous process. When physical confrontations arose, they turned into ghastly or mysterious crimes. If an aggressive government servant or a business lobbyist attempted to break the social discipline enforced through policing, governance and social kinship and climb into the party through subterfuge, they could end up in a different kind of crime. Outsiders were not taken kindly in that society, even though it was now being led by those who were once among the 'revolutionaries'.

There were several scandals involving jeeps and ammunition – the best of which were manufactured only abroad. Then there were scandals involving agricultural items – jute, clarified butter and even jaggery. In 1950, industrialist Ramkrishna Dalmia caused a public uproar by claiming that the government's policy regarding jute export had caused a loss of Rs 30 crore, a mighty sum in the prevailing circumstances. This was followed by the 'Ghee Scandal Case',[8] which alleged that two military officers and twelve businessmen had connived to secure a contract to supply ghee worth Rs 1.8 crore to the government.[9] The issue persisted even before the demise of Prime Minister Jawahar Lal Nehru. *The Times of India* reported on 5 March 1964 that three ministers – Gulzari Lal Nanda, Swaran Singh and Asoke Sen – defended the government's handling of the 'gur scandal' in the Lok Sabha.[10] At the core of the controversy was the price at which gur (jaggery) was sold by the Central Co-operative Stores of Delhi in November–December 1963. The three ministers argued 'no favour was shown to any person, howsoever high-placed he might be'.[11] However, these cases and debates around allegations of involvement of persons from the ruling party did not unnerve the prime minister personally. It was the Mundhra scandal of 1957 that threatened Nehru's impeccable image. The well-documented case ultimately led to the resignation of Finance Minister T.T. Krishnamachari, the biggest political shock to the Nehru years. One final case that exploded in the last months of the Nehru government was the 'Serajuddin affairs' that had roots in the diary of a businessman. Like the 'fertiliser case', the 'Serajuddin affairs' also had roots in central-level politics but had their lead characters in Orissa and West Bengal. The case stretched back from 1951 to 1956. As Prime Minister Nehru passed away, intense bickering broke out among Congress stalwarts like Biju Patnaik and Biren Mitra.

In the midst of this situation, there were rumours that H.N. Sanyal, the Solicitor General of India and the highest-ranking legal officer of the government, was examining some documents related to the Orissa affair. Sanyal was widely recognised as an erudite scholar of law and had moved to Delhi during the peak of the Mundhra scandal in 1957. He took up residence at 22 Akbar Road, which was near the residence of Prime Minister Shastri at 1 Janpath. His immediate neighbour was Lok Sabha Speaker Hukam Singh.

Sometime after midnight on 8 September, Sanyal's security guards heard noise from his bedroom, and it appeared that four persons were assaulting him. His servants were roused from their beds because of the unusual commotion. By the time they walked into his room, the four assailants had left the property, and the Solicitor General of the Government of India had been smothered to death. That the Solicitor General of India, who was referred to as a 'graft hunter' by *The New York Times,* could be killed in the heart of the power elite of Delhi showed the poor state of security in the Indian capital. The uproar caused by the murder did not go away, and on 15 March 1965, Praja Socialist Party (PSP) member S.N. Dwivedi tabled a motion expressing a lack of confidence in the government of Prime Minister Lal Bahadur Shastri. *The Times of India* on 16 March recorded that it was the second time that a censure motion was tabled in Parliament in a span of nine months since Prime Minister Lal Bahadur Shastri succeeded Prime Minister Nehru. Shastri had an impeccable personal reputation for leading a frugal lifestyle but Dwivedi was not targeting him personally. He said by the handling of the Serajuddin affair and the allegation of corruption at the state level, Prime Minister Shastri had lost the 'moral authority to rule the country'.[12]

2

The King of Aliases and His Queen

When Chittoor Venkat Narain, a man whose life story and career as a middleman were yet to unfold, stepped onto the platform of Kashmiri Gate railway station in 1949, it marked the beginning of a new chapter in his life.

The distant whiff of coal stoves wafted into the railway compartment, followed by the aroma of freshly brewed milk tea that woke Coomar Narain up. Outside the Kashmiri Gate railway station, a mixture of scents such as burning coal stoves, freshly brewed tea and tobacco served as a wake-up call. India had gained independence, and the railway platforms became the first supermarkets where consumer goods, books and smuggled items from American soldiers returning home were found. Until then, he had only seen the name of the capital on envelopes that he handled at the post office in the Kamptee military cantonment. In his bleary vision of that winter of 1949, he saw the city that had become a part of his life in the past few years when he worked as a postal clerk in the military.

The first thing that caught Coomar Narain's attention on the railway platform was the sound of the coal engine hissing. Interestingly, the steam engines were not built in India. Like most items used in the country, the steam engines were imported as Indian engineering companies did not have the licence to produce them. Narain arrived in

Delhi on that early, bleary morning by train, in the city that would become his future workplace, where he would work as a consultant-general manager in a major engineering company. However, at that time, he only caught a dark, smoky glimpse of the entrance to the city.

Delhi was being mobbed by humanity. The previous year, a considerable population had arrived as refugees as the Partition gave shape to the new country. Coomar Narain was just one of the men coming into the capital. How was the city that welcomed Coomar Narain?

Coomar Narain joined the Government of India as a stenographer and in the summer of 1949 became a permanent resident in Delhi. Although he had visited the city before, he did not expect to stay there for the rest of his life. However, Coomar Narain had a unique feature that set him apart – he was not comfortable with just one name. Like Delhi, which is known by various names, such as New Delhi, Indraprastha, Hastinapur and Delhi, Narain also appeared with different names, including Narayan and Narayanan. But eventually, his second name, Narain, became more widely recognised.

Coomar Narain was fiction. Chittoor Venkat Narayanan was the reality.

That is what Shiv Dev Singh from the Economic Offences Wing of Delhi Police learned when he started looking into the files. The Delhi Police approved his travel plans in the summer of 2017, and he boarded a flight to Kozhikode. Once he arrived, he found out that Coomar Narain, who had been involved in an espionage case before, was again at the centre of a police investigation. However, this time, it was a property dispute involving characters who had passed away several years ago. The life of the infamous character would be unveiled before Shiv Dev as he met with people who were initially hesitant to see him and searched obscure documents in dusty government offices. As he delved deeper, he discovered more about the life of this infamous character.

Shiv Dev's first stop was Vadakkencherry to inquire about Coomar Narain, aka Chittoor Venkat Narayan. However, he found no information from the office of the local sub-divisional officer and district magistrate of Palakkad. According to them, there was no record of Chittoor Venkat Narayan's family in the area, and nobody knew his father, Venkitarama Aiyar. Migrants usually do not leave any traces behind, which are anyway eventually erased by time.

Shiv Dev, a Gurgaon-born Haryanvi, felt exhausted due to the constant language barriers in the villages around Chittoor. These villages were home to the Palakkad Iyer community, a Tamil-dominated enclave within Kerala. The Palakkad Iyers originally hailed from this place. Shiv Dev visited the agraharams and temples of the Iyers, but he was in civvies and had to introduce himself as a police officer in every conversation. Unfortunately, the interaction would break down each time he revealed his Delhi Police ID card. Upon reviewing the information in the chargesheet of the case he carried in his briefcase, Shiv Dev discovered that Coomar Narain had grown up in Coimbatore. So he decided to travel to Coimbatore by bus. It was from Coimbatore that the Iyers had departed for Palakkad, where they had been granted refuge by the Zamorin of Kozhikode many centuries ago.

Coimbatore in 1925, when Coomar Narain was born, was vastly different from the Tamil Nadu city of 2017. The houses that once stood there had been replaced by high rises and markets. Additionally, roads had been widened where there were previously only little alleys. However, this expansion did not make finding of Venkitarama Aiyar any easier for Shiv Dev.

Based on the age given at his death in 2000, Coomar Narain was probably born in or around 1925. His father Venkitarama Aiyer had moved from Palakkad to Coimbatore,[1] where Coomar Narain spent his childhood. Shiv Dev searched through the alleys of the old quarters in Coimbatore to find clues about the Narains but was unsuccessful. It seems his extended family found him intimidating because of the reports of his success in Delhi, and gradually drifted away as Coomar Narain focused on his fractured life and prospering career.

During the Second World War, C.V. Narayanan attained majority and moved to an army cantonment near Nagpur, where he received training in the Army Postal Service from 1943 to 1947. Kamptee,[2] a colonial town near Nagpur, was a beautiful place to start a career. Shiv Dev also visited it, an important colonial-era location for intelligence operatives, as it was the operating base of the Army Postal Service. Soldiers and spies sent many letters through Kamptee due to the war in Europe and Southeast Asia. As a result, important information passed through the area, which was viewed with interest. It is unclear whether Coomar Narain was introduced to the ways of the intelligence world here while he handled letters from the front. Did that kindle a sense of curiosity in the world of professional intelligence officials? It is not known definitively. But it is known that a few years later, his career would bring him into the confluence of trade, technology, lobbying and Cold War–era intelligence. His training in the postal service hinted that Narain probably was not a stranger to the intelligence network of colonial India during the declining years of the Raj.[3]

The war was raging outside, and cities like Calcutta and even Allahabad were within the range of Japanese bombers. However, Nagpur and Mumbai were far from the conflict. In Kamptee, civilian postal workers sorted the mail of soldiers, ensuring that their families received their correspondence. Coomar Narain was not only a postal department worker but also an intelligent person. Despite his humble and soft-spoken nature, everyone in his surroundings knew he was the most educated person on the floor, with an MA in economics.

When Coomar Narain was arrested in 1985, the incident gave the impression that he was a college graduate with connections with lower-level clerks. However, records from the army show that he only completed high school. Despite this, he received a 'war medal' for his service, and his character at the time of discharge was 'very good'.[4] Coomar Narain worked in the same profession till 16 July 1949 when the army stated that his 'service no longer required'. After his discharge, Coomar Narain left for Delhi to start a new future in the new capital of free India.[5] There are reports that suggest Coomar Narain's decision to travel to Delhi was impulsive, but he had already seen the city when the Army Postal Service transferred him from Kamptee to Ambala shortly after 1947.

As the train approached the city, Narain finally caught a glimpse of the city of many illusions. Despite the smoky odour of burning dung cakes emanating from the villages along the rail tracks, there was the illusion of enormous success in this unknown city. Outside the station, Delhi was infested with diseases and decay, but just beyond the smell of urine, there lay a life that beckoned every visitor to Delhi in the late 1940s. The city's heart was dark, rickety and full of ancient lodgings that were either painted white or had fallen into disuse. The houses of Kashmiri Gate exuded the aristocracy of the past century, but there was little sign of prosperity in them. The entire area was melancholic. Compared to Bombay, which he had seen earlier, the city seemed small.

As Coomar Narain began to settle into the city, he discovered a new side to it. After dark, the area from Kashmiri Gate to Darya Ganj came alive with laughter from people who were not visible during the day. Coomar Narain recognised some familiar aspects of Delhi in the South Indian restaurants and eateries of Old Delhi. The area was also home to a strong Christian community from Goa and Mangalore, as well as Anglo-Indians who lived nearby. Each group had its own watering holes, such as the Bengal Club, the Goa Club some distance away in Panchkuian Road and the Punjabis, who had come in large numbers from western Punjab in recent years and made friends to enter the clubs tagging along with other friends. Coomar Narain discovered the Goa Club through his Christian friends in the military and was enchanted by its old, quaint interior. He also noticed that there was a lot of his native Kerala in this part of the stretch, with many churches and graveyards belonging to the Christian community. The English-language schools run by the Christian missionaries attracted many good stenographers from Calcutta, Goa, Kerala and Bombay, who filled the central government positions at the clerical level. It was during his military days that Narain was introduced to the opportunity for jobs at the central government.

He carried the tales of Chittoor in Kerala in his DNA, the birthplace of Brahmins like him. The Iyers were a diligent and aspiring community of workers who aimed to climb the aspirational social ladder through education and hard work. They were known to be faithful and honest to their employers. Coomar Narain had worked in the armed forces, but his job was civilian in nature. It was part of the short service commission, initiated to support the war efforts. Early media reports from 1985 suggest that after coming to Delhi, Coomar Narain worked in the Ministry of External Affairs. However, police records show that he worked in the Department of Economic Affairs. It is possible that he was transferred from one ministry to another during the decade he worked as a stenographer in the central government.

Coomar Narain worked for the Government of India during the 1950s, but details of his service are sketchy and mostly found in reports that came long after he had left the government. Clerks were expected to bring their skills to the service, but little investment was made in nurturing their talents. The more fortunate elite services were trained better and sent to foreign locations with the best facilities. However, clerks were treated poorly.

The grand corridors of the South Block exuded a magical quality. Here, the powerful appeared even more powerful and the powerless insignificant. The powerful and privileged seemed legendary, but the lesser mortals were reduced to irrelevance. However, this was not true for the clerks and section officers in the same building. Coomar Narain, in particular, proved to be dynamic in his role. In the coming decade, he repeatedly tried to break free from the limitations that the role of a 'clerk' had imposed on him.

In the years leading up to his arrest, Coomar Narain amassed a substantial amount of wealth. However, despite his wealth and influence, he never gained acceptance into the inner circle of the powerful. His social circle included those who were less privileged, such as government officials like himself at one point. Despite being an outsider to the circle of power, Coomar Narain had access to information about the government machinery and knew everything that was going on behind closed doors. It is possible that his desire to remain informed and involved in the centre of power is what kept him on the outside, looking in.

Looking back, one can only imagine the trepidation a junior section officer or stenographer may have felt in the South Block, which the ICS officials and the new elite of post-colonial India heavily dominated. Did Coomar Narain feel a sense of inferiority while walking in the same corridor? Did he feel he was not as polished as the top officials with perfect English diction? India's hierarchical bureaucracy is such that the top order rarely interacts with their subordinates, which can be detrimental to the morale of lower officials. In the early 1950s, stenographers were likely to feel neglected compared to the privileged officials of IFS and the leaders. It may have been in these circumstances that Coomar Narain's timid personality was shaped.[6]

In the 1950s, the newly independent India was creating films about Indian villages, tales of reincarnation, youthful love, the triumph of the human spirit over poverty and exploitation and religious themes. However, no one really considered section officers or clerks in government offices as a subject for a landmark film. The small desks of stenographers, their lunch boxes and their world of fearful submission to their more powerful superiors were all part of this small universe. High officials would wear expensive ties and perfumes, but stenographers like Coomar Narain wore white half-sleeved-shirts and grey-black trousers, dressing suitably to reflect the marginal existence that they led. Ostentatious displays would be frowned upon and could make their survival in the office difficult. Politicians and bureaucrats would turn out in crisp fabrics, but stenographers would wear tailor-made half-sleeved shirts and flowing trousers with buckles procured from Meher Chand Market. It would take some courage for a stenographer to sport a formal jacket.

Some stenographers were luckier and more enterprising than others. One such rare person was M.O. Mathai, the private secretary of Jawaharlal Nehru. Mathai, a Syrian Christian from Kerala, was from the same part of India that also produced Coomar Narain. He not only became the stenographer of the first prime minister of India but also became some sort of influencer in the official circles. Mathai travelled with the prime minister and claimed to have interacted with the guests and visitors who came to meet Nehru.[7] Over nearly two decades, Mathai served Nehru in pre-Independence India and then became the legendary secretarial assistant known as 'Mac'.

The stenographers and secretaries formed a distinct social class. They were privy to confidential information, phone numbers, meetings and salacious gossip. Mathai, who belonged to the same class, shared their worldview, which was based on the norms prevalent in the 1950s and 1960s. Despite their knowledge and opinions, they held no significant position in the system in which they worked. At the height of the License Permit Raj, stenographers who lived on the fringes of the government had access to classified information in various ministries. Coomar Narain showed that stenographers were more than just typists who mechanically took dictation and supported the officials. Although they remained largely unnoticed by high-ranking diplomats and administrators, they could make use of the information they possessed to make money, provided they chose to break the moral code that enveloped them like a net.

It was evident that Coomar Narain of Coimbatore/Chittoor was no match for the public school boys and the erstwhile princes who had joined government service after India gained independence. While Coomar Narain had decent speaking and writing abilities,[8] he lacked the key to success in the newly established India. In order to be successful in the new India, he needed to innovate and change. Like Mathai, he did not possess good looks either. However, Mathai was more anglicised than Coomar Narain, which enabled him to climb the ladder of power. Coomar Narain wanted to break free, but he was all too aware that he did not have the strength to break the invisible chains holding him back. While his language skills were not in question, as a Tamilian from the South, his Hindi remained imperfect until the end of his life. Nevertheless, Delhi was a city of opportunities, and Narain perhaps found those opportunities outside his government office in the realm of business and politics.

Hiding within the more than thousand-page archive of Coomar Narain's personal life, which is in possession of the Delhi Police, is a page that sheds light on a turning point in his life as a government servant. It was the year 1958, and the owner of a house in Nizamuddin East, which was a newly developed neighbourhood meant for the cultural elite of the capital, wanted to sell his house to a lady named Joyce. According to the document, Joyce, a native of Mysore, was staying at Kashmiri Gate 'c/o O. P. Bahl'. It was the first time that Bahl, who was then beginning to climb the political ladder of the ruling Congress party, was introduced in the voluminous documents related to Coomar Narain. The political figure would have an interesting career in the next two decades, lasting exactly as long as the heyday of the Congress party till the end of the Emergency rule of Indira Gandhi. Shiv Dev maintains that Joyce was, in fact, the sister of the woman who was set to marry Coomar Narain. This is the same property that drew interest from Coomar

Narain, who, for the first time, appears as 'C. Narayan' in a document dating back to 1957 for the same property in Nizamuddin Extension – C33-A. It is this property that was then claimed in 1966 by Geetanjali Narayan in 'mutation'.

In the late 1950s, Chittoor Venkat Narayan began introducing himself as C. Narayan. It is unclear when the name of Narain became C. Narayan and when the C came to denote Coomar, an Anglicised version of 'Kumar'. One legend suggests that an astrologer advised Narain to change his name or that he changed it when he started working as a corporate lobbyist for a Bombay-based firm. However, it is clear that all the names belonged to Narain. He used so many aliases that even his death certificate does not carry his real name. The only name that stuck was Coomar Narain, which became well-known during the cold January of 1985.

If Narayan, to be Coomar Narain, was an aspiring stenographer who was aiming for a future in business liaising and lobbying, there were his contemporary colleagues in other segments of life as well. More prominently, they were in politics. Chaudhry Brahm Prakash, Radha Raman, Kishore Lal, Lala Shyamnath and Om Prakash Bahl emerged as frontline local leaders who provided support structure to people arriving in the city to make it big in Nehruvian India. These notables were not top-of-the-rung leaders. They provided the people with a connection to the political elite and were essential in the corporate-politics interface in Delhi. These local-level mobilisers of the Congress party were handled by the likes of Subhadra Joshi and Aruna Asaf Ali, among others.[9] They were also divided into camps based on who in the top level of Congress leadership handled them. Coomar Narain wanted to get close to them. Coomar

Narain's aspiration to earn big money required that 'people connect'. He could not do it himself. He required a partner. Bibiana Gerty Walder provided that connection.

In 1943, when Coomar joined the postal department of the army, Bibiana Gerty Walder or B.G. Valder or Gerty Valder alias Gerty D'Souza became a young, unwed mother to a young child in Mangalore. The restless youngster, however, abandoned the baby with her mother, Juliana, and moved to Delhi. There are different theories about how she met Coomar Narain. Gerty worked in a firm in Bombay and came to Delhi after meeting Narain, who had visited Bombay for work. Another theory suggests that Coomar Narain met Gerty at the Goa Club on Panchkuian Road.[10] Yet another suggests that Gerty was working as a secretary for a Chikmagalur politician who had an important role in Delhi and brought her to the capital.

In the only surviving photograph with her husband, she is seen standing beside him. Both of them are in their advanced years. The husband appears happy, but the woman has a tense expression. Although Coomar Narain did not leave behind written documents, his wife did. She appears to write coherently without grammatical mistakes when urging the banks regarding joint accounts and properties.

In other photographs, Geeta Narayan can be seen with ferocious dogs, her favourite companions. She appears in Coomar Narain's life suddenly in legal papers in 1966. The house that was sold to Joyce is hers. Mrs Narayan appears as 'G.N. Mangalore' as well as Geetanjali Narayan and Geeta Narayan in property-related papers of the Narains from the 1960s to 1970s. Why she had three different names is not explained in any official documents. Like Coomar Narain, whose name changed multiple times over thirty-five years, Geeta also changed her name frequently. Despite her petite appearance, Geeta was ambitious and assertive, and there is no doubt that she was the stronger half of the Narains.

Assertive and strong-willed, Gerty was meant for something bigger than Mangalore. Her stronger presence and firm voice intimidated men.

Neither Coomar Narain nor Gerty knew that Delhi would become the chosen city of their lives. But the decision to settle in Delhi took shape as Coomar Narain got a job in the Ministry of External Affairs and left his military service. Gerty was strong-willed, had charisma and was a head-turner. Venkat was educated and ambitious. Gerty was Christian and Venkat was a traditional Tamil Brahmin.

The two complemented each other. Coomar Narain understood that Gerty could provide him with the kind of support he required to navigate the government sector of the 1950s. They were both running away from their past, but their chance meeting led to a mutual understanding of the importance of their alliance for self-preservation. Coomar's frenzied life and career later revealed that marrying Gerty, or Geeta, was the first major business decision he made. Coomar lacked the ability to cultivate politicians on his own; that responsibility fell to his vivacious wife. Gerty was more than just a wife to Coomar; she was a business partner who deserved reverence.

They knew very little about each other. Perhaps the only thing that brought them together was the fact that they were both strangers in the Indian capital. Sometime in the 1950s, Coomar Narain decided to marry Gerty D'Souza in order to fast-track his life. This was a major business move that would transform Chittoor Venkat Narayan into the more sophisticated-sounding Coomar Narain. With this marriage, Gerty shed her Christian identity and became Geetanjali, while C.V. Narayan embarked on a new, uncertain, but challenging phase of his life. There is also a theory about why he changed his name.

Venkat and Geeta consulted an astrologer from Chennai to know about their future after marriage. The astrologer predicted that the couple was destined for great things, but Venkat had an obstruction in his path. The astrologer suggested that Venkat had to change his name to taste success. Venkat took the letter 'C' from Chittoor and combined it with a royal-sounding North Indian name, Kumar, and thus he became Coomar Narain. Soon after, Coomar Narain learned that SLM Maneklal, a Mumbai-based engineering firm, was looking for a liaison officer in Delhi. He decided to make the transition from his government job to SLM Maneklal in 1959.

The couple moved to C-33A Nizamuddin, where many artists and poets lived after their income increased. By the mid-1960s, they had overcome their struggles. Geetanjali Narayan, also known as G.N. Mangalore, legally owned the house in Nizamuddin.[11] The astrologer had also asked Geeta and Coomar to have children as soon as possible. In the initial years, Coomar focused on his job as a liaison officer for SLM Maneklal.[12] His job had the potential to bring in a lot of money, and his personal life helped him make important political connections in the city that initially intimidated him. Coomar Narain had finally tamed Delhi's political and corporate landscape.

Coomar had a strong entrepreneurial spirit that thrived in his job. His company had assigned him a challenging task, which involved leveraging the friendships he had built within the government over the course of the decade between 1949 and 1959. Geetanjali and Coomar Narain were an ambitious couple from Delhi whose ill-fated lives were perhaps best suited for the world of intelligence. Unbeknownst to them, they had shed all their original identities and created new ones to match their aspirations in the Indian capital.

3
Signs of the Enemy

Over the last several years, New Delhi became more open to the world by welcoming numerous diplomatic missions filled with activist diplomats, intelligence officials and local liaison officers. This elevated New Delhi's global stature but also made the city vulnerable to new threats that had not existed before. These missions had a special requirement to be present in the Indian capital, the centre of power in new India, under a government that adopted decolonisation as a national policy. The government gave the impression that India did not want adversarial relations with anyone and wanted to balance relations with the Soviet- and US-led blocs. India tried to cultivate friends on all sides of the global divide. It occasionally performed certain activities that raised suspicion in the eyes of the global centre of power in the West. Soon after India's independence, the Nehru government did something that raised the West's suspicion about India's real motivations.

Nuclear physicist Weldon Bruce Dayton passed away at the age of 101 in 2020. His death not only marked the end of a remarkable phase of India–US relations but also broke a significant link to the shadowy world of espionage during the 1950s. During one of his visits to the United States, where he had many friends, including Albert Einstein, Homi Bhabha, the father of the Indian atomic programme, met Dayton and invited him to work at the Tata Institute of Fundamental Research in Bombay. Dayton was known to have been part of the group that included Julius and Ethel

Rosenberg, who were executed for nuclear espionage in 1951. Theirs was the highest-profile espionage case in the world at the time it was uncovered.

In the autumn of 1952, Dayton received a letter from his friend Bernard Peters. Peters, a student of the legendary Robert J. Oppenheimer, informed Dayton that Dr Homi Bhabha, Director of Tata Institute of Fundamental Research, would be visiting Chicago and would like to meet him during his trip. Peters was already employed with Tata Institute of Fundamental Research and the institute had acquired global fame because of the research being carried out by the scholars there. The discussion from that point led to the Tata Institute of Fundamental Research offering Dayton a job at a salary of Rs 120. Although Dayton was a skilled cosmic ray theorist, the US State Department suspected he was part of the Rosenthal espionage ring, a group of physicists with leftist leanings. As a result, the US State Department withheld his passport. The tussle between Dayton and the State Department continued for most of the decade. Dayton disputed these allegations and swore that he had never been a member of the Communist Party. Still, the State Department maintained that he could potentially 'advance' the Communist movement if he were allowed to go to Bombay.[1] The legal battle continued for most of the decade until Dayton was eventually able to travel to India to work at the Tata Institute of Fundamental Research.

For a newly decolonised state, India's quest for nuclear energy was a symbol of self-respect. Canada, a fellow Commonwealth member, supported India's nuclear energy programme by sharing technology and reactors.[2] However, New Delhi's strategic choices were a mix of good, bad and questionable decisions. India was a member of the Commonwealth but also a friend of Egypt, which

was on the brink of a confrontation with the UK. In 1955, Egypt's leader Gamal Abdel Nasser visited India, and soon thereafter, a team of five Egyptian scientists visited the country's atomic energy institutions.[3] India was not a hostile country, but its ambitions in various fields made it a target for foreign espionage. Despite the bitter experience of colonial exploitation, India maintained cordial relations with Great Britain and the West, as well as with other postcolonial states. Although India was friendly to all sides of the global divides, it knew it could encounter an enemy in the future.

The Dayton episode in India was a clear indication that the country was serious about technology and willing to take on the most powerful nations in the world to access it, thereby multiplying the power of the Indian state. India's aim was not to resurrect a mythical past but to build a future rich with technology. Therefore, the country was ready to challenge the dominant powers in the world to gain access to it. However, a little over a decade later, tragedy struck as the *Kanchenjunga*, a Boeing 707 aircraft belonging to Air India, crashed on Mont Blanc at 7:02 am. Unfortunately, among the 117 passengers who lost their lives was Dr Bhabha, the most widely travelled scientist of India and the father of the country's nuclear programme.

The Dayton episode and the US government's reluctance to share high-calibre scientists with India marked a significant moment in India's technology history. From the outset of its independence, India had displayed a keen interest in acquiring cutting-edge technology for both its public and private sectors. However, India had to deal with espionage concerns that came from global players as much as from its neighbour, the newly born rival power – Pakistan.

Every enmity has its weight, and the enmity with Pakistan shaped India's mind with a good dose of paranoia.

This began soon after India gained independence, and the first war with Pakistan took place in October 1947. Prior to this, India's intelligence operations had focused on varied challenges, such as revolutionaries in Bengal in the early 20th century and communications with Japanese and German operatives in Berlin and Tokyo. However, the creation of Pakistan through a bloody partition and the subsequent bitter war of words over the possession of Kashmir, Junagadh and Hyderabad brought to light a deep-seated anxiety. Pakistan's demands created an instantaneous revulsion, and India responded strongly, but it had adopted Panchashila as the pillar of its foreign policy and it was not going to exhibit its darker side so soon. Nevertheless, there were moments when the dark side was exposed.

In 1949, the Government of India faced embarrassment when a Pakistani news outlet revealed a discriminatory order by the Indian government. The central government had issued a secret circular to all the states, in which it pointed out that several Pakistani citizens were employed in critical industries, such as oil fields, steel works and other critical industries. The underlying message of the order was that these jobs were meant for Indian citizens, and organisations employing Pakistani citizens could very well employ Indian citizens instead. Additionally, the order hinted that employing such a large number of people from a hostile neighbour may not be wise, especially during an emergency situation.[4] Unlike Pakistan, India aimed to be an inclusive society, and the news embarrassed the government of Prime Minister Nehru. At the same time, it was revealed that a blueprint of an ordnance factory from India was sent by post to Pakistan. Although the information sent across the border was not of great importance, it indicated internal weaknesses that the Indian security establishment had to be concerned about.[5]

The story of a network of section officers in multiple ministries and the Prime Minister's Office became the talk of the town thirty years after India started recognising the role of clerks and section officers in modern intelligence operations. In this context, two cases became notable for introducing section officers to the intelligence-gathering process in the Indian context.

In 1954, the world was a dangerous place. On the one hand, the Cold War blocs were reshaping the world, and on the other hand, India aimed to ensure neutrality as a foreign policy goal. Later in the same year, Pakistan joined the South East Asian Treaty Organisation (SEATO), which it formed along with the US, France, UK, Australia, Philippines, Thailand and New Zealand. This brought dangerous Cold War dynamics to South Asia, which was yet to recover from the ravages of the Partition of 1947 and internal problems like food insecurity and endemic poverty. In the summer of 1954, newspaper headlines announced the spy scandal of Rehmat Masih–John Mathew Gill and Corporal Rangia. Masih was a clerk at the local branch of the Bible Society, John Mathew Gill was allegedly a Pakistani CID officer, and Corporal Rangia worked at the Indian Air Force headquarters in Delhi. Masih and Gill were working at the behest of a Pakistani diplomat stationed at the High Commission in New Delhi. Gill and Masih befriended Corporal Rangia and began to collect information through him. But before long, they were exposed and arrested after Corporal Rangia became an approver in the case.

After the clerk, it was the turn of a section officer. In 1956, Shadi Lal Kapoor, a section officer in the Ministry of External Affairs, was suspended from his job. It was claimed that he had supplied official documents to 'foreign agents'[6]. This happened during a time when the cult of the middleman had become established in the Indian capital, along with the story of an aspiring city. However, the case fell apart soon after it was discovered that Shadi Lal Kapoor's confession was extracted under custodial torture. This case is illustrative of the fear and paranoia that often existed parallel to India's claims of enlightenment while leading the newly decolonised countries of Africa, Asia and Latin America.

The 1950s were a time of fear and suspicion, especially for India. Having gained independence in 1947, the country was concerned about its security due to its rocky relationship with Pakistan, which had joined Western military alliances. India was suspicious of Pakistan's intentions and feared the friendship of Pakistan and Western countries. It was in this condition that John Foster Dulles, US Secretary of State, visited New Delhi in March 1956 to meet Prime Minister Jawaharlal Nehru. During his visit, Dulles attempted to dispel India's fears about Pakistan despite being the source of fear and paranoia. He held lengthy meetings, attended a dinner at the Rashtrapati Bhavan and went to bed with a glass of milk. Although Delhi was beginning to open up to the world, it was more welcoming to the Asian and African countries than it was to the West. When Dulles left, the American community in Delhi, which numbered only 200, bid him farewell.[7] However, the interaction with Dulles did not alleviate Delhi's fear, and the city became increasingly anxious about the unknown. The new enemies were Pakistan and China, and India viewed several stakeholders with suspicion.

The medieval Indian empires, including the Mughals, were familiar with espionage and intelligence operations. However, in modern India, these age-old concerns have re-emerged in a completely new avatar. New Delhi was a bustling city with a central shopping district, diplomatic enclave and new residential areas where people from different parts of India came to reside and work in the government and private sectors. This influx of people brought with it the potential for fear and unpredictability, which lurked in least-expected street corners and neighbourhoods.

It was in this condition that a businessman in Karol Bagh was raided by the police. The allegation was of supplying documents to a country in Europe as well as a 'leading communist country'.[8] These activities became intense in the backdrop of the military setback of the Sino-Indian War of 1962 when the search for the enemy within became the new normal. Nearly a year after the war with China, the case came to light. On 3 September 1963, a pilot officer in the technical branch of the Indian Air Force named Prakash Narain Sharma was arrested for violating the Official Secrets Act. He was accused of passing secret documents to the Pakistani Air Attache in Delhi. Sharma was tried by an Air Force tribunal at the Red Fort and was given the maximum punishment of fourteen years under the Official Secrets Act. Sharma served his sentence in a civil jail. His case was the most prominent of a series of cases involving similar allegations. In one case, an employee of the Ministry of Defence was accused of passing documents to Pakistan. In another case, a group captain of the Indian Air Force was dismissed from service in August 1963 after it was discovered that he had been sharing information with a foreign power. Three back-to-back cases involving allegations of links between hostile powers triggered curiosity in the media. The media was curious about the third case involving the group captain, as the foreign power in question was not named. In the previous two cases, the foreign power was expressly mentioned as Pakistan.[9] Was the foreign power, in the case of the group captain, a friendly country? Was India now being subjected to espionage even by friendly countries? The fear of the unknown and an enemy began to infest India's security domain.

Over the next two decades leading up to the mid-1980s, espionage activities in the Indian capital gradually evolved. However, the 1960s and 1970s were far more dynamic in terms of events, with diplomats often being the focus of bizarre incidents that were not always thoroughly investigated. In 1970, Sheikh Hussain Bin Mohammed Al-Suleiman, a Saudi diplomat who lived in the Civil Lines neighbourhood of Delhi, was found murdered along with his teenage domestic assistant, Gabriel. The investigation seemed to ignore the possibility that the injuries inflicted on the diplomat could only have been possible if it was carried out as a revenge attack or to settle a vendetta. It was quite possible that the domestic assistant heard his master's screams during the attack and was eliminated when he was spotted by the intruder.

The incident, which received sizeable media attention at that time, reached a curious solution when Daniel Krishnaswamy, the driver of the Saudi diplomat, was arrested from a hotel in Bombay's Marine Drive. According to the prosecution, Daniel claimed he killed the diplomat after he was denied permission to use the official car for an errand. According to him, the diplomat had asked him to do the day's shopping, but Daniel insisted on taking the car out to the market, which he denied. The diplomat promptly dismissed the driver from his job. Police insisted that the driver killed the diplomat as a reaction to this incident. Yet the explanation of the eleven stab wounds on the diplomat and his cook did not make sense, but the investigators did not probe it any further.[10]

But the most bizarre espionage-related story came in 1978 during the case of the brutal murders of two teenage siblings,

Sanjay and Geeta Chopra. Infamous murderers Ranga and Billa, also known as Kuljeet Singh and Jasbir Singh, were blamed for the twin murders. The siblings had taken a lift in a car from Dhaula Kuan to go to All India Radio. The car's owner was a prominent doctor who dropped them off a kilometre from the radio station on his way to his clinic in Connaught Place. The children were supposed to reach the radio station to participate in the popular programme 'Yuva Vani', but they went missing instead. Their father Captain Chopra later found their bodies and the crime was blamed on Ranga and Billa, who were reportedly hardened criminals that kidnapped children from wealthy families and demanded ransom. However, the murder left several unanswered questions, and there were several theories that the crime was committed as a message from some sinister forces.

It was reported that a seaman who was convicted of smuggling and served a seven-year jail sentence held a grudge against Captain Chopra, who worked at the office of the judge advocate general's branch. Another possible angle was related to an espionage scandal that took place in 1974. It was rumoured that several officers of the Indian Navy were punished for their involvement in espionage and that they worked for a powerful international agency of the 'communist bloc'.[11] According to a report published by the *Times of India*, the 'murders were a warning to senior naval officials by the espionage networks'.[12]

It is worth noting that none of the spy scandals mentioned earlier could match the impact and range of the Coomar Narain spy scandal, which was the biggest spy scandal of its time and has remained unsurpassed in terms of the frenzy it generated. When the scandal broke out, the media focused on the so-called 'spymaster' Coomar Narain. His life of luxury was recorded in detail and his taste for wine and women was routinely presented in the media. However, questions about who Coomar Narain was and who his employer, SLM Maneklal, remained unanswered. It is surprising that these questions were never explored in full detail.

The scandal had multiple aspects, some of which were questionable while others were legitimate. The sensational headlines of the spy scandal overshadowed the personal struggles and life-changing experiences of many individuals involved. However, two additional parts of this scandal were equally intriguing and presented a complete picture of the men and women involved. These included the corporate entity that was swept away in the tumultuous currents of sensationalism and the city of Delhi that provided a conducive environment for unsavoury developments to unfold.

The scandal in Delhi did not explore the city's political underbelly for its malevolent potential. Instead, the headlines were fixated on Coomar Narain's alleged wickedness. It would take years for other incidents, such as the Naina Sahni murder and the helicopter scandal of Romesh Sharma, to expose the elaborate, ruthless network that networkers ran in the national capital. While news columns mentioned the Maneklals of Bombay as part of the scandal, there was no exploration of who they were. Therefore, it is important to turn to the remarkable history of the SLM Maneklal, one of the most pioneering engineering companies of mid-20th century India, and its rise and fall. The story will begin with the first signs of a turn in the tide.

4
The Company

In 1974, Gujarat witnessed a political upheaval that was inspired by the ideas of a colourful politician, journalist and filmmaker, Indulal Kaniyalal Yagnik. Yagnik started his career as a filmmaker and a follower of Mahatma Gandhi, but after independence, he became a critic of Prime Minister Jawaharlal Nehru. While being a member of the Congress, he maintained a maverick streak and formed a trade union called Sangram Parishad,[1] which organised a major textile strike to demand higher bonuses. The strike was a success and Yagnik's actions inspired others to follow his example.

The event of 1974 was preceded by months of distress across India. Inflation had skyrocketed and unemployment had ruined the dreams of the masses across India. The situation was no better in the rest of India, where Indira Gandhi's socialist policies had brought the country's economy to a near halt. The government was forced to seek help from the World Bank and the International Monetary Fund for a financial lifeline. The International Monetary Fund granted the loan but also imposed strict conditions. The situation became volatile as public anger grew. The government in Delhi was becoming increasingly unpopular, leading to the spectacular fall of Indira Gandhi, who had been celebrated and described as Goddess Durga just four years earlier after the Indian victory in the Liberation War for Bangladesh.

Gujarat was under the rule of Chief Minister Chimanbhai Patel, who had risen to power due to his abilities and not because Indira Gandhi chose him. However, the chief minister's unpopularity matched the growing national unpopularity of Indira Gandhi. The problem started in January of 1974 when the students of Gujarat protested against the high price of essential commodities. The state was already tense, and the students provided the trigger for which it was waiting. The Nav Nirman Yuvak Samiti led the movement and was perceived as being steered by fiery student leaders Manishi Jani and Umakant Mankad.

The entire state erupted and law and order broke down. Shops were looted, homes were broken into, government property destroyed and the police stood by stunned. The breakdown was so widespread that the government machinery was overwhelmed. During the university examinations of 1974, a farce played out when teachers requested students not to indulge in violence with folded hands, and the angry students were allowed to copy and consult each other while writing answers. The universities and authorities were worried about the students' behaviour and were willing to go to any extent to placate them. Despite all these extraordinary measures, the students walked out of examination centres several times, protesting against 'difficult questions'.[2]

The people of Gujarat were demanding the resignation of their chief minister, Chimanbhai Patel. Indira Gandhi, the prime minister of India, saw this as an opportunity to remove Patel from his post and promptly dismissed him. However, the protests continued and transformed into a larger movement for political regeneration known as Navanirman. The people were now demanding the entire Congress-dominated legislature be sacked. After several days of protests, Indira Gandhi gave in and the MLAs of the Gujarat assembly resigned. Later, the Government of Prime Minister

Indira Gandhi accused foreign forces, specifically the Central Intelligence Agency, of being involved in the unrest.[3]

During this time of the disturbances in Gujarat, the industry suffered and companies faced challenges. One such company was SLM Maneklal, a prominent manufacturer of engineering equipment and engines. One of its plants in Ahmedabad had to be closed for two months due to the turmoil. This was the first setback for the thirteen-year-old company caused by unexpected external factors. The Navanirman movement, which triggered larger unrest against the Indira Gandhi government, was a defining factor in Indian politics. This led to the declaration of the Emergency in the summer of 1975, which impacted a large swath of politics and business. The disturbances caused by Navanirman were completely unexpected by the all-powerful Indira Gandhi government, let alone by SLM Maneklal, which was focused on expanding its business at the time. Despite the setback, the young company did relatively well. Sales for the year ending in March–April 1974 were higher than the previous year, at Rs 3.07 crore, but gross profit was down from Rs 74.64 to Rs 68.72.[4]

SLM Maneklal, which repeatedly made headlines due to its bold approach in the engineering industry, was not the pioneering part of the Maneklal dynasty. That role was played by the patriarch of the family, Trikamlal Maneklal.[5]

The story of the Maneklal dynasty began with Trikamlal Maneklal Chamdawala's birth on 7 March 1911 into a well-to-do Jain family of Ahmedabad. Mr Maneklal acquired his primary and secondary education in Ahmedabad and began his college education with 'zeal and ambition'[6] against the backdrop of the intensifying struggle for freedom in India. Like many of his generation, Maneklal's educational ambitions were disrupted by the Gandhian freedom movement.[7]

But Trikamlal Maneklal was a person who did not let the lack of formal education get in the way of his ambition to earn a living. He discovered his life's calling at an early age and started his professional journey by working in the millgin stores on the western coast of India. The millgin stores in Gujarat and Maharashtra were critical to the textile industry, as they supplied fabric and essential equipment for textile mills and merchants. These stores played a vital role in setting up textile mills and provided maintenance-related services for the factories. Textile mill owners relied on millgin stores to set up their manufacturing business and continued to depend on them for as long as their manufacturing unit functioned.

T. Maneklal was a young and ambitious person who dreamed of creating a mega store that would supply all the necessary items for the textile sector. He wanted to design his company as a one-stop destination for all the products required by the textile mill owners. The first product that T. Maneklal introduced was a versatile rubber roller, which was a critical component in the textile sector. He aspired to expand his business beyond the textile sector because rubber rollers were also required in other industrial sectors, such as paper mills, textile, iron and steel units and more. T. Maneklal's clientele was expected to spread across the United Kingdom, Africa and the Arab world.[8]

After his initial years of struggle, T. Maneklal started his entrepreneurial journey in 1941 with a small workshop.[9] Despite the challenges posed by the Second World War and the already weakened economy of India, he boldly established a company that manufactured rubber products for the industrial sector and the general public. The company also produced rollers for cotton and silk textiles and paper industries.[10] Additionally, it manufactured rubber items that were essential for surgical procedures. The company was producing items for which there was high demand in the Indian market.

After India gained political independence, T. Maneklal's confidence was boosted. A year later, on 7 December 1948, the organisation became a public limited company and received a certificate to manufacture on 9 January 1950.[11] Prior to this, T. Maneklal's company only produced smaller items such as rubber drums, gloves and rollers for the textile sector. However, they decided to aim big and started manufacturing machines, specifically textile machines, for bleaching, dyeing and finishing. During a decade that was marked by war, famine and political assassinations, T. Maneklal went from working in the millgins to setting up a manufacturing company for the industrial sector – an achievement that was rare for his time. In 1948, the company operated from Parel in Bombay, but soon thereafter, it built units and sheds in Sakinaka, Kurla–Andheri Road and Mohli village.[12] T. Maneklal had achieved his dream in a remarkably brief period of time with sheer determination and focus, and he passed this impatience to excel to his sons, Suresh and Yogesh. By 1958, Suresh had become the managing director of the company and was helping his father in managing the growing manufacturing business.

T. Maneklal dreamt of building his company into the best manufacturer of industrial machines. He wanted to supply factories with the equipment they needed throughout their lifetimes. The father-son duo and other senior employees of the company travelled to Europe to connect with the best industrial machinery builders.

In 1954, the company achieved a major breakthrough when it entered into its first foreign collaboration with Benninger of Switzerland to manufacture automatic jiggers.

In 1957, the company collaborated with Benninger again to manufacture chainless cloth mercerizing machines marketed under the brand name 'Benninger–Maneklal'. During this time, the company also entered into a partnership with Swiss Locomotive and Machine Works of Winterthur Switzerland to produce rotary compressors. T. Maneklal Manufacturing Co. Ltd also became the 'sole concessionaires' in India for the goods manufactured by Swiss Locomotive and Machine Works of Switzerland. Swiss Locomotive and Machine Works manufactured locomotives, diesel rail cars, lightweight rail cars, brake compressors, brake vacuum exhausters, pump sets, roots blowers and more.[13] The Swiss partner received 10,000 equity shares as payment. SLM Maneklal began production in India and acquired 2 lakh square yards of factory land with plans for acquiring 1 lakh square yards of land in addition. It received assurance of a steady electricity supply and planned to start production in December 1962. This move made the Maneklals a part of the big league and was highly lucrative.

The Maneklals were the success story of independent India's engineering industry. They were the new stars of India's small but fledgeling private sector. The Maneklal family was prosperous and known to live as a joint family. Although they were not as big as the Tatas or the Birlas, they were among the notables in Bombay and commanded attention. The family events and developments in the company were covered in newspapers like the *Times of India*. They were not known for attending high-profile parties or social gatherings but were keenly followed in the media, both on business pages and in city news.

On 8 December 1961, the *Times of India* announced that T. Maneklal Manufacturing Company had established a new company called SLM Maneklal Industries with a manufacturing facility located in Vatva near Ahmedabad. The company had been set up to produce 'high horsepower diesel engines'[14] ranging from 163 HP to 655 HP. The estimated output was 45 engines per year per shift, with plans to increase to 75 engines per year per shift. The establishment of this new company was an ambitious venture of the T. Maneklal Manufacturing Co., aimed at helping the younger generation of the Maneklal family to establish themselves in the engineering sector. From the media reports garnered in its initial years of existence, SLM Maneklal appeared to be young, ambitious and aggressive.

Patriarch Maneklal realised that in a state-dominated economy, direct access to the ruling party in Delhi was essential. He understood that political links with the ruling party were necessary to support his business acumen. Accordingly, he brought Congress luminaries onboard his ventures. This is evident in the newspaper reports and advertisements that the Maneklals placed in the *Times of India*, Bombay edition, during their prosperous years in the 1950s, 1960s and 1970s.

Jaykrishna Harivallabhdas, a prominent industrialist of Gujarat, not only led the Congress but also became part of the company's political connections. With the arrival of SLM Maneklal, the political influence of the company grew more prominent as Jayakrishna Harivallabhdas became the chairman of SLM Maneklal, and father-son duo T. Maneklal and Yogesh T. Maneklal worked as managing directors. The arrival of the company generated media headlines soon after.

SLM Maneklal was a prominent company closely monitored by reporters in the economy beat. The company's activities were frequently covered in the 'City Notes' section of *The Times of India*'s Bombay edition. In fact, the media extensively covered the company during its active years, providing enough information to create a precise timeline of its projects and public announcements.

Matching aspirations, SLM Maneklal had a wide scope of activities, which included holding public meetings, sponsoring events and announcing job vacancies. These activities reflected the aspirations of the company. Within a year of its announcement as part of the T. Maneklal group, SLM Maneklal showed great promise. By the winter of 1963, the company had acquired the sole selling agency of Sulzer Brothers of Switzerland for India.[15] The factory in Vatva was ready within a year, and all the imported machinery was acquired without any government restrictions. The trial productions were scheduled to begin by the end of November 1963, and commercial production was planned to start by December.[16]

In 1972, an advertisement in *The Times of India* read, 'Imagine 5000 mouths blowing all at a time – A single SLM Maneklal Rotary Air Blower does that'.[17] The company also advertised its role in the plastics industry, showcasing plastic pipes, bags and containers. The company's history of foreign technological collaboration, which began with Swiss Locomotive and Machine Works often recorded in its ads or newspaper reports. By 1985, according to Yogesh T. Maneklal, the company had collaborated with twelve different countries.

A decade after its inception, SLM Maneklal was growing rapidly and being led by Yogesh T. Maneklal who believed that foreign collaboration was necessary to maintain the company's reputation of 'precision engineering'. On 7 May 1971, SLM Maneklal published a public notice in a newspaper announcing 'that in pursuance of Section 25 of the Companies Act 1956 and application has been made to the Government of India for a licence declaring that a body about to be formed under the name of the Maneklal Scientific Research Foundation'.[18] The foundation was, however, expected to work as a company as per the declaration, which stated that it was created to undertake, conduct, carry on or help to carry on scientific research for the extension of knowledge in the fields of natural and applied science.[19] The notice was advertised to draw public attention and stood out as a unique venture with the approval of the company's leaders – Trikamlal Maneklal, Yogesh and his brother Suresh.

Yogesh T. Maneklal was aggressively marketing his company as a technologically advanced entity. He was willing to invest in research to stay ahead in the race. In January 1971, T. Maneklal Manufacturing Co. Ltd launched two joint ventures – one in Nigeria and one in Canada. In Nigeria, T. Maneklal Manufacturing Co. Ltd partnered with Messrs. Kaycee Lagos to establish a textile weaving and finishing plant. Additionally, T. Maneklal Manufacturing Co. Ltd set up a factory for hand-printing textiles in Canada.[20] According to the newspaper records from that time, the company focused on new initiatives and foreign collaborations at every step. It did not display any weakness till the external disturbances from Navanirman impacted it.

In the summer of 1974, the company faced a setback. However, due to its strong foundation, the company was able to recover quickly. As SLM Maneklal continued to pick up foreign collaboration, history was inching closer to them. During the Navanirman movement, public disturbances began and Indira Gandhi declared the Emergency rule to contain the situation. But Maneklals managed the political situation well and stayed ahead of the curve. In 1976, at the height of the Emergency, Maneklals reported that the Rexroth–Maneklal arm of the company, promoted by younger brother Yogesh T. Maneklal but led by elder brother Suresh, was going to enter the capital market.[21] G.L. RexrothGmbH, a German major, collaborated with Maneklals to produce hydraulic equipment for the Indian market. This was a timely move and Maneklals captured a major chunk of the market quickly. The Maneklals were at the height of their glory, riding on the twin engines of Suresh and Yogesh. However, the stability of the Emergency was to end soon, and so would the golden phase of the family, as a shadow would enter their lives.

Unlike the big business houses of that time, like the Tatas, Wadias and Birlas, the Maneklals did not have a past going back to the peak of colonial rule. They were a product of the Swadeshi movement that started with the call given by Mahatma Gandhi. The industrial house was started by Trikamlal Maneklal in his youth, catering to rubber, dye and colours for the textile industry of western India. Unlike the older and much bigger industrial houses, they did not have the proximity to the colonial rulers or the blessing of the nationalist leaders leading the freedom struggle. However, they learned that to survive in the Indian business scene, they had to cultivate the right connections. They also realised that overseas partnerships were crucial for their success. These partnerships were a way to acquire foreign partners and access the best of both the West and the East. For Maneklals, it was a bold venture that took them to Poland, the USSR, East and West Germany, the US and France, but one that could turn against them in case of a security factor. T. Maneklal Industries Ltd was set up by Trikamlal Maneklal Chamdawalla in 1941, at a time when Poland sent Jewish refugees to Gujarat, where the ruler of Jamnagar gave them refuge. In the next decade, Maneklals would tie up with the famed Polish shipping companies to bring their expertise to India.

Maneklal was appointed as the Indian representative of the Swiss Locomotive and Machine Works. The company was supported by local businessmen and political leaders. However, in the early 1950s, private engineering firms faced a major challenge in acquiring technology. The hunger for technology shaped engineering firms like SLM Maneklal. This was an expected problem for post-colonial India. During the colonial period, there had been little industrial development and even less technological production. This meant that companies had to look elsewhere for technology, either by innovating through trial and error or by relying on 'experienced foreign collaborators'.[22] The latter option led to dependency and was not ideal.[23]

SLM Maneklal opted for the second option and became a prolific partner-seeker in the field of technology acquisition. According to a 1984 publication by K. Balakrishnan from IIM Ahmedabad, the company initially sought Indian partners. It teamed up with Jyoti Limited, a local engineering enterprise from Ahmedabad. In fact, companies of that era were paying the price of the technological gap that existed between India and the West. Till the Second World War, India depended on the import of Western machine tools,[24] and the same became a template even as private sector players blossomed in Nehruvian India. However, Nehruvian India was also providing these companies with new opportunities. Every industrial or agricultural project, from drought-prone north Indian plains to factories that required water and other liquid materials, required pumps. Pumps were placed in tube wells and factories from Uttar Pradesh to Gujarat. SLM Maneklal first began to import pumps and then began to manufacture them. During this time, it also teamed up with Jyoti Ltd. Interestingly, Jyoti Ltd, founded by a dynamic engineer, Nanubhai Amin, continues to operate as a leading private sector engineering company, whereas SLM Maneklal, one of the first batch of major engineering firms of Nehruvian India, is now reduced to a phantom of history.

Looking back, it seems almost poetic that SLM Maneklal's success as an engineering company began at the same time as the blueprint of its future. Technology had been a crucial factor in strategic intelligence, as evidenced by the production of nuclear weapons by the United States and the Soviet Union. The acquisition or transfer of technology always carries a risk when it comes to long-term security. However, if the company had relied less on imported technology, it could have avoided what was prevalent during the Cold War era. Despite this, SLM Maneklal became a chosen partner of several leading companies, such as Poland, West Germany, Switzerland and others, over the three decades since its founding.

In 1975, the World Bank conducted a survey of textile processing machinery and named SLM Maneklal as the 'largest' producer of 'processing machinery' for the sector. The report stated that the company produced 75 per cent of both 'dry and wet processing machinery'.[25] The textile industry was rapidly growing in India, and four or five leading machinery makers were supported by foreign collaborators to cater to the growing Indian market. According to a World Bank report, Maneklal produced fifteen different items, including 'stenters, jiggers, mercerisers, fibre machine, spray towers, rubber blankets' and other items required by textile mills in Bombay and Ahmedabad.

Maneklal was not the only player in the processing machine sector that served the textile mills. There were other companies as well, such as Swastik Bansidhar Engineering Pvt Ltd, Calico Industrial Engineers and Famatex India

Pvt Ltd. These companies emerged in the immediate post-Independence period when India's industrial policy started attracting enterprising engineers and technological genius from established companies. The government's broad policy determined the focus areas of these companies. During the first five-year plan, the government focused on food production and in the second plan, it shifted its focus to power projects and electrification. This increased opportunities for the production of basic industrial items. India was a new country, and its industrial policy catered to a brand new economy's demands. The initial industrial demands of India were primarily focused on agriculture, textile, mining and defence-related items. Therefore, tractors, watches, switches, pumps, vertical pumps and industrial capacity pumps for factories and ships were some of the early items that drove India's industrial engine.

While taking up the Coomar Narain case, it is therefore important to understand that he was not responsible for creating the means of espionage, but rather he took advantage of an opportunity presented by the industrial requirements of post-Independence India. The government promoted foreign collaboration, training and education with an eye to building domestic capacity and Jyoti Ltd played a crucial role as a 'machining subcontractor'[26] for SLM Maneklal. Nanubhai Amin, who was trained in post-war West Germany (Federal Republic of Germany), shaped Jyoti Ltd's vision of foreign collaboration, which was focused on the requirements of technology or engineering companies at the time. In its early years, SLM Maneklal and Jyoti Ltd produced squirrel cage induction motors and pumps, which were in high demand due to the irregular municipal water supply across the country. Joint ventures with foreign collaborators provided a steady supply of cash, with a 5 per cent royalty on sales assured as per the standard Indian procedure laid down by the government. This collaboration involved the exchange of know-how, drawings and other relevant details but did not cover 'licences or patents, pre-investment services, machinery and plant construction, training and transfer of personnel and periodic solving of unexpected problems.'[27]

In 1965, the Monopolies Commission recorded SLM Maneklal as a manufacturer of 'diesel engines, roots blowers, water ring pumps'. Vacuum pumps work on the principle of suction, which is created by a vacuum inside the device. The principle of suction can be used to transport fluid or gaseous ingredients on the factory floor. The company produced pumps for various industrial sectors, and with the intensification of industrialisation in India, the demand for vacuum-based pumps increased. SLM Maneklal was well placed to fulfil its role in the fast-changing Indian scenario.

Gujarat, one of India's western states, underwent an economic transformation that created a demand for industrial capacity pumps. The pumps were required by both the textile and defence sectors of India, and the Maneklals were able to capitalise on this expanding market. While the engineering products from the SLM Maneklal company catered to multiple sectors like pharmaceuticals, irrigation and petroleum extraction, over time the company became more associated with the defence industrial sector. It is worth noting that pumps, especially vacuum pumps, were essential in establishing any industry.

During the 1960s, in the industrial climate, there were rules that required government approval for any initiatives that involved foreign entities and the flow of capital. For this assignment, the company chose an address located centrally in Delhi, which was 16 Hailey Road. The house was one of the oldest structures on Hailey Road, dating back to the early

20th century when New Delhi was being designed and built by Edwin Lutyens and Herbert Baker. The house had both colonial and traditional Indian styles with tall, sturdy pillars and a large garden in front. The Aggarwals who owned the property came from an engineering and construction background and had participated in the building of New Delhi. SLM Maneklal rented an office space on the right side of this prestigious location. The front of the house was for the owners, and the firm's outlet could be accessed through the door that went inside.

It was this location that Coomar Narain was expected to turn into a trijunction of bureaucracy, foreign embassies and his corporate masters.

Coomar Narain's entry into SLM Maneklal was not a landmark event, but his departure would later make history for the company. Coomar Narain's confession was immediately sealed, so his corporate resume cannot be accessed. However, veteran journalists Vinod Sharma and the late G.K. Singh of *The Week* magazine, along with other reporters who wrote about the Coomar Narain case in the 1980s, chronicled that he had worked for SLM Maneklal for nearly twenty-five years at the time of his arrest. Although the exact tasks performed by Coomar Narain for SLM Maneklal are unknown, the allegations of his interactions with certain countries match the projects that were part of SLM Maneklal's corporate profile. Coomar Narain was accused of having links with diplomats and intelligence officials of certain countries, and SLM Maneklal also had interaction with those countries. It may not be incorrect to assume that Coomar Narain had professional reasons to get close to the embassies of France, Poland, East Germany and the Soviet Union, as these were the countries that were of interest to his employer, who often sourced their technology partners from them. What added to the drama around Coomar Narain was the claim that he had been active for twenty-five years.

The job of a lobbyist could be carried out by someone who had a good understanding of the social network of officials in the ministries important to SLM Maneklal. Coomar Narain's past work experience was therefore of interest, as he had started by working in prominent ministries such as the Ministry of External Affairs[28] and the Ministry of Finance.[29] Over the years, Coomar Narain had become known not only as the mastermind behind a quiet network that operated in the heart of the government but as someone with access to six European embassies, specifically France, the German Democratic Republic (East Germany), the Federal Republic of Germany, Poland, France and Switzerland – all of which were crucial countries for SLM Maneklal. In the 1970s, SLM Maneklal had emerged as the sole Indian representative for Unitechna of Berlin, German Democratic Republic and provided 'complete plants for the production of nylon and acrylic fibres'.[30] Similarly, Centromor of Poland, Benninger of Switzerland and Kautex of West Germany, which produced plastic blow moulding machines, required careful investment planning and surveying of government policies in India. These projects provide a glimpse into the kind of paperwork that Coomar Narain had to deal with.

It is possible that given the powers that sponsored his work, Coomar Narain had to travel abroad on several occasions during his service. There were also media reports indicating that he underwent some form of intelligence-gathering training.[31] While there is no concrete evidence of Coomar Narain's training in the field of intelligence, it is known that he was briefly posted in the Indian embassy in Beijing during his service as a stenographer in the government.[32]

5

Temples, Ships and Military Secrets

In 1985, there were 2000 liaison officials working for various corporate entities in India.[1] Scattered across Delhi, Bombay, Calcutta and other major cities, they had survived during the first four decades of post-Independence India. Coomar Narain was one of these 2000 professionals, yet he was the one who hit the headlines and remained the favourite of newshounds for a long time. There was something unique about this soft-spoken man who obviously had an elaborate network of friends and well-wishers, yet had remained unknown to society at large. At the beginning of the case, it came to light that nearly eighteen individuals, mostly from within clerical ranks, had been arrested, and another 188 witnesses were cited by the prosecution.[2] The information network did not prove charges of espionage, but it was impressive nevertheless, as it indicated that Coomar Narain had a friend in nearly every minister's office that mattered and, most importantly, in the Prime Minister's Office and the office of the president of India. Having so many friends in so many diverse setups required a long and efficient stint.

After the arrest of Coomar Narain, K.C. Sharma, an Indian working at the World Bank, was summoned from his job in Washington, DC. He arrived in Delhi on 6 March and was arrested on 12 March. Sharma had previously worked with an official of the shipping and transport ministry.

During his conversation with the investigative officials, he revealed that he had known Coomar Narain for the past decade, going back to the mid-1970s and had shared official documents with him. Sharma was the eighteenth person to be arrested in the case. This arrest was particularly noteworthy as it demonstrated the longevity of Coomar Narain's relationship with his government sources. He was not a fly-by-night operator. Coomar Narain was a trusted and dependable individual who was regarded as someone who could be entrusted with official documents.

A similar long-term association was also seen with Jagdish Tiwary, another of Coomar Narain's contacts who was arrested. Both of them were government stenographers and had been friends since 1958. Coomar Narain left the government job while Jagdish Tiwary continued working. After three decades, the only progress that Jagdish Tiwary had made was eventually becoming a senior stenographer in the Department of Economic Affairs.

In the three decades before his arrest in 1985, Coomar Narain had acquired multiple properties and had become wealthy. On the other hand, Jagdish Tiwary remained in the same socio-economic segment. Despite their different paths, whenever they met, Jagdish Tiwary would get a glimpse of the comfort that Coomar Narain had achieved. Coomar Narain's commercial information gathering stretched back in time to the late 1950s and the 1960s, which he accomplished by building solid social connections with his colleagues and friends. His skill set did not involve high technology, but it was his affection for his friends and former colleagues that helped him maintain a formidable network for information gathering.

This was seen most clearly in the case of P. Gopalan. He was an employee in the Prime Minister's Office and regarded

Coomar Narain as a father figure. In papers submitted to the passport office, Gopalan had said, 'in case of death, inform Coomar Narain'.[3] Coomar was a father figure to his friends and former colleagues, a successful man who had worked his way up from humble beginnings in the Indian capital. However, there were questions regarding his personal life that needed answering. How did Coomar Narain maintain his friendship with so many people for many years? Was it just the lure of wine and sex, as the news reports suggested? Or was there a more socially acceptable form of engagement that Coomar Narain used to maintain his friendships?

Coomar Narain's personality was shaped by his private life and beliefs. Although he was not much into religious activities, he used religion to connect with many of his contacts in various government offices. South Delhi underwent a religious transformation during the post-Nehru years, with an increase in the number of godmen and ashrams in farmhouses. Big temples with rare marble were built as religion made its presence felt in the Indian capital. The bureaucrats were known to support the religious events in the temples of Delhi and temple committees often invited noted Vedic scholars from places like Kanchipuram for elaborate rituals. These special ceremonies were attended by the entire community, including government officials. Coomar Narain was a regular attendee of some of these events, which helped him maintain his social network, as many government officials also frequented these temples.[4] One prominent south Delhi temple even published a souvenir that carried an advertisement from SLM Maneklal, a clear indication of the close relationship between Coomar Narain and the president of the temple committee, who was also from Tamil Nadu.[5] Coomar Narain relied on simple and time-tested methods of social engagement to build his social network over twenty-five years as a corporate lobbyist in the Nehru and Indira years. He did not depend on sophisticated technology, which meant that he did not come under the radar of law enforcement authorities as his behaviour was socially acceptable.

After the arrest of Coomar Narain, media reports surfaced with sketchy details about the profile of SLM Maneklal. However, most of these reports made little sense. The company was supposedly involved in foreign collaboration and used it to earn from foreign intelligence agencies. In reality, foreign collaboration was a long-standing practice of SLM Maneklal. The real espionage was more complicated than that. In an attempt to reinvent itself, the company signed an agreement with Weatherford of Houston, Texas, to enter the offshore oil exploration and extraction business.[6] Weatherford specialised in tools and equipment for complete oil field services for exploration and production of oil and natural gas.

India had embarked on major industrialisation in the 1950s, and industrial families like the Maneklals seized the opportunity. The units producing engineering tools were thriving and SLM Maneklal was a success story in those early days as India expanded its defence sector, which also boosted the industrial base. Soon after signing the deal with Weatherford, SLM Maneklal entered into tie-ups with Uniroyal of the US and Manauli Danadanio of Italy for rubber and belting equipment. In little more than a decade, the company prospered and boasted some of the biggest government agencies and ministries among its clients.

It was discovered that SLM Maneklal supplied various public sector companies[7] in India with defence-related rubber products, as well as the Department of Atomic

Energy and the Bharat Heavy Plate and Vessels Plant at Visakhapatnam. Documents found with Coomar Narain showed that SLM Maneklal had an order for helium refrigeration equipment from the Department of Atomic Energy and a refrigeration unit from Bharat Heavy Plate and Vessels in Vishakhapatnam. Additionally, it had an order for Selzer column packings for vacuum distillation for the Rasayani-based[8] Hindustan Organic Chemicals.

Coomar Narain was gathering inside information for SLM Maneklal's legitimate manufacturing work. In India's public sector-dominated system, a manager with the capacity to lobby with insiders was necessary. Coomar Narain provided the Bombay-based Maneklals with exactly that. The details of Maneklals' rise are shrouded in mystery. In 1985, investigative journalist Ashok Row Kavi reported that in August 1984, Yogesh Maneklal told reporters that his company had submitted tenders to Oil and Natural Gas Corporation Limited for the supply of goods and services for Rs 7 crore. But after January 1985, both Maneklal and Oil and Natural Gas Corporation Limited said that the tenders were for Rs 3 crore only. The discrepancy of Rs 4 crore was not explained. According to intelligence sources cited by Kavi, the missing amount was a payment from the Central Intelligence Agency, United States, to the company, which was laundered for offshore exploration[9] and drilling. While the involvement of the Central Intelligence Agency in the Coomar Narain network remained unexplored, there was ample proof of it in media reports of the case.[10] Intelligence agencies of France, the Soviet Union and diplomats of Poland and East Germany were also named at the time of the discovery of the Coomar Narain network.

Indian intelligence agencies suspected that exploration for oil required a large amount of money, and Maneklal

Industries Ltd used this route to launder the cash that was received as payment for information gathering. It was reported that both the US and the USSR also used similar methods to launder cash into India for their specific purposes. The USSR allegedly did this through the infamous rice supply contracts for the country.[11] However, Maneklal Industries Ltd did not have to wait long to get their big break. It was Poland, not the Central Intelligence Agency, who played a crucial role in helping Maneklal Industries Ltd.

In 1972, Raj Kapoor launched his son Rishi Kapoor and a teenager named Dimple Kapadia in a smash hit love story. The film portrayed the two characters as madly in love in the midst of disapproving parents from diverse political and economic backgrounds. Dimple Kapadia sang 'Prem Rog' as she hugged the hero tightly. The film became a sensation and Dimple Kapadia and Rishi Kapoor became the heartthrobs of millions of Indians. The third beneficiary was the bike that they rode, the sturdy Rajdoot. Without the lovers on that bike riding on the mountain road, *Bobby* would not have been that big a hit. It was a dream for many young people, and the bike stole India's heart. Originally named SHL M11, the bike was built in Poland and rebranded in India as 'Rajdoot'. The Escorts Group of Delhi launched it in the 1960s. It was a Soviet-era machine that was tough, durable, exuded masculinity and adjusted to the rough Indian roads easily. Polish bikes and scooters put out advertisements in Indian media showing women riding Polish scooters and men riding SHL bikes. India's cooperation with Poland reduced after the Cold War, but for the first three decades of independent India's existence, Poland was a name that evoked trust and friendship in the hearts of India's struggling industrial class, which looked for technology transfer on easy terms.

In the realm of international developmental partners of India, Poland had a significant and lasting impact on SLM Maneklal's agenting business, particularly through the efforts of Coomar Narain. However, as the years went on, Coomar Narain's agenting would cause trouble for the company.

In 1961, Poland's largest state-owned shipping company, Centromor, appointed SLM Maneklal as its sole trade representative[12] in India, a position that would last for the next two decades. Centromor was established in 1950 and quickly became one of the three major shipping companies in Poland. It soon began to cater to clients as large as the Soviet Union, the Union Kingdom, Norway and other major naval powers in the world. During the 1960s and 1970s, Coomar Narain's job was instrumental in fostering the prosperous maritime relationship between Poland and India, with SLM Maneklal serving as the sole trade representative for Centromor in the country. The Polish company put up large advertisements in shipping magazines in India to highlight SLM Maneklal's special status with the company. In addition to being a trade representative, SLM Maneklal was also known for making vacuum pumps. As a trade representative, the main task of SLM Maneklal and its chief representative in Delhi, Coomar Narain, was to ensure a steady flow of commercial contracts for the Polish company in India, which translated into a hefty commission for the company as it was their agent in the country.

After the Second World War, Poland began building ships under its newly independent leadership. The war had severely impacted the Polish economy, including the shipping industry. However, with renewed independence, Poland turned to shipbuilding as a way to strengthen its foreign relations, particularly with countries like India that had a high demand for maritime expansion. Poland excelled in shipyard repair and constructing ships, as well as various ship components. Coomar Narain was able to succeed in his work on the ground thanks to the excellent bilateral and multilateral diplomatic ties between the leaderships of Poland and India.

In 1955, Prime Minister Nehru visited Warsaw, where he and Josef Cyrankiewicz, Chairman of the Council of Ministers of Poland, issued a joint statement. Poland supported India's relationship with Beijing, giving a boost to the diplomatic ties between the two nations. Nehru and Cyrankiewicz found common ground on neutrality and non-interference in the domestic affairs of sovereign state members of the United Nations, which further strengthened their relationship. This helped in crafting industrial policies in India that supported the growing industrial sector of the country.[13] The diplomatic warmth between India and Poland continued for the next two and half decades and throughout his career, Coomar Narain and SLM Maneklal served as the unofficial ambassador for Centromor.

Coomar Narain worked in Delhi for the Centromor–SLM Maneklal combine, which held exhibitions promoting Polish shipping expertise across the country.[14] In 1959, 1961 and 1968, Poland showcased its shipping industry in Delhi and organised promotional events. In collaboration with SLM Maneklal, the Polish company held major social events attended by political and industrial notables of the License Permit Raj under Indira Gandhi.[15] These events were crowded with contract seekers and embassy hoppers seeking good food and wine. Small films promoting Poland were shown in these events, which were organised in prime locations in the city.[16] The maritime or shipping trade was part of the overall Poland–India trade during 1955–66, when trade between the two countries increased twenty-nine-fold.[17] One of the main reasons for the rapid growth of Poland–India trade during the 1950s,1960s and 1970s was the economic reality of India, which was a struggling economy that looked for trading partners through strategies like 'assistance through trade'. The root of this strategy was the need to conserve the precious foreign currency of the country and barter commodities with developed countries in the West. At the height of the Cold War, when industrial cooperation was difficult with the West, the Eastern Bloc countries provided valuable support to India. The Eastern Bloc nations, consisting of socialist economies like Poland, the German Democratic Republic and the Soviet Union, among others, provided India with the option of barter trade. This kind of economic and industrial cooperation helped the socialist economies find clients in the developing countries, while the developing countries could preserve foreign currency reserves. Coomar Narain's footprints can be found in Chennai, Ennore, Mumbai and Kolkata, where Polish companies assisted electric projects, shipping and the transport sector.

The Polish dockyard was the go-to choice for shipbuilders in India. Ship parts were custom-made in Warsaw and shipped to India. Coomar Narain played an important role in making this dream a reality. Poland's marine footprint spread from Gujarat to Visakhapatnam, along the Indian coastline, providing support to the shipping industry.

The advertisement featured a model in traditional Indian attire, showcasing a fabric line called 'Fabrics you love to wear – Rollin–Maneklal Rubber Blankets are indispensable for their printing'.[18] The advertisement caught the attention of textile producers on the west coast of India who needed them to print beautiful sarees in their mills. The blankets, an essential item for manufacturing textiles, were previously imported from France. It was manufactured by the French company Rollin. However, T. Maneklal Manufacturing Co. Ltd collaborated with the French company to produce them locally in India. Rubber blankets were not only required in textiles but also in polyvinyl chloride and metal sheet production. The Maneklals assured their customers that the rubber sheets would be made to their specific industrial specifications. Rollin was the first French connection of the Maneklal company that was publicly advertised to attract customers. It was a world-renowned company producing rubber blankets for the manufacturing sector, and the rubber sheets were a must-have for big fabric mills and other industries.

However, the announcement was made in the name of T. Maneklal Manufacturing Co. Ltd. It was apparent that the SLM Maneklal branch of the family business had secured collaborations with Poland and Switzerland, while the T. Maneklal branch had partnered with French. During the 1960s and the early 1970s, the Rollin–Maneklal collaboration made steady progress, with the peak of T. Maneklal Manufacturing Co. Ltd, under the leadership of Suresh T. Maneklal, occurring in 1970. *The Times of India* reported 1969–70 as an 'excellent' year for the company, with turnover surging from Rs 1.90 to Rs 2.73 crore.

Maneklals were astute in sensing commercial opportunities in the economies of third-world countries.

Egypt provided them with one such opportunity. At this time, T. Maneklal had been lobbying to secure export contracts with the United Arab Republic (comprising Egypt and Syria), Czechoslovakia and Sri Lanka. It was also the time when the company began to lobby with the German Democratic Republic for export orders of its machines. Additionally, it received an 'important bulk contract' from the Ministry of Defence of Indira Gandhi's government.[19] Suresh had reached the golden phase of his company, and from this point onwards, it began to slow down a bit. However, the story of Yogesh T. Maneklal was only beginning.

In April of 1973, SLM Maneklal of Yogesh T. Maneklal made an important announcement. The company was partnering with Japan's Toshiba to herald the plastic revolution in India.[20] The collaboration led to the creation of Toshiba–Maneklal plastic injection machines, which are widely used in India to produce plastic items of various sizes. The machines were used in both large and small industrial facilities for many years. The Maneklals, especially SLM Maneklal, were known for seeking out foreign collaborations, having worked with companies from capitalist West Germany to socialist Poland and neutral Switzerland and Austria.

The story of the Maneklal brothers reveals some internal differences and rivalries between them. Both brothers were in charge of different sections of the company that complemented each other, but Yogesh had made his mark with his bold business moves over the previous two decades. In just one and a half decades, he had established SLM Maneklal as a force in the market. In the biggest move of that time, Yogesh T. Maneklal brought Toshiba into the market in 1973 and introduced the Toshiba–Maneklal plastic injection moulding machines to India. The company's advertisements in national newspapers announced the partnership to the world. There was little doubt that in the third decade of the company's existence, Yogesh had become the face of the Maneklal group with his fast moves that revived the sector of precision engineering. Yogesh was fast catching up to his elder brother and positioning himself as his equal after the temporary jolt that was delivered to the company during the Navanirman phase in the summer of 1974. Signs of distress were to soon emerge. Beginning in 1973, Yogesh had begun to receive greater responsibility.

After the peak of 1970, Suresh, the elder brother, made some bold moves. One such move was to enter into an agreement with Kaycee Lagos to set up a textile unit in Nigeria. At the same time, Yogesh T. Maneklal rose to the highest post in the company. On 1 August 1972, SLM Maneklal announced in the newspaper that the Board of Directors had requested permission from the Government of India to appoint Yogesh as the managing director of the company.[21]

In October of the following year, the company announced that both Yogesh and Suresh would serve as managing directors of T. Maneklal Manufacturing Co. Ltd from 1974 to 1979. However, major political developments were taking place in India and in June 1975, Indira Gandhi imposed the Emergency rule. A month later, the Board of Directors of T. Maneklal Manufacturing Co. Ltd cleared the post of managing director for Yogesh T. Maneklal till 1979. Meanwhile, something else was happening far away from the company's headquarters in Bombay that would change several destinies in the next decade. Yogesh T. Maneklal's destiny was to be among them.

In the early 1980s, Sri Lanka experienced ethnic conflict between the Sinhalese and the Tamils. In 1983, an anti-Tamil riot occurred in Colombo, which brought intense focus on the situation in the island country. India was drawn into the crisis, which caught the attention of Indira Gandhi. Against this backdrop, the Indians and Sri Lankan officials were supposed to meet in Delhi for a confidential discussion. However, as the meeting began, Sri Lankans confronted the Indian team with a top-secret R&AW document that gave Colombo a hint of what was the thinking of the Indian Prime Minister's Office. It was an embarrassing situation. The intelligence officials were surprised as the document that the Sri Lankans had come with was written just for the top Government of India figures. There were only three sets of that document. Two sets of that document were circulated internally in R&AW, and the third copy was shared with the Prime Minister's Office. There was considerable curiosity in finding out how the top-secret document reached Colombo. It was eventually discovered that a French official had shared this document with the Sri Lankans through the Coomar Narain network.[22] Although it is difficult to know the precise details of what Coomar Narain did for the Maneklals during the previous twenty-five years, it was understood that he knew several important people in diplomatic and security circles. None of his sources were new acquaintances, and he had known them for years. The Coomar Narain network's specialty was collecting documents, but they had no control over the end use of the information.

Coomar Narain had his own methods of maintaining his social network, which was crucial for information gathering. He used to shower an abundance of paternal affection upon the men and women who came in contact with him. Those who were close to him were given expensive gifts, which he bought from a well-known showroom in Connaught Place.

He also had a favourite sweet shop in Bengali Market, from which at least two of his contacts were allowed to buy as much as they wanted on his account.[23]

The scale of the Coomar Narain network was mammoth. At the beginning of the trial, at least 188 witnesses were summoned, most of them government officials who had met Coomar Narain.

6

Nicobar

Like wine, high fashion and fighter jets, luxury perfumes were one of the quintessential identities of France. However, not long ago, counterfeit and illegal perfumeries in Asia were causing millions of dollars in losses for French perfume brands. This was made possible due to the duty-free status of places like Singapore. Local businesses imported essential chemical ingredients from France or Switzerland and packed them in glass bottles imported from Taiwan. The final products were nearly identical to the original ones produced by brands such as Yves Saint Laurent and Pierre Cardin. The counterfeiters almost took over the market of the original Yves Saint Laurent perfumes. The duty-free shops that promoted French perfumes in Southeast Asia had begun to pose an existential threat to the original perfume makers. In 1987–88, an estimated 800,000 bottles of fake perfumes of Yves Saint Laurent were exported from Singapore.

Unable to deal with the perfume pirates through normal commercial processes, Yves Saint Laurent employed a special security director to combat the counterfeiting. The security director sought the help of both government and private investigators to track down the illegal perfumeries that produced fake perfumes. These illicit groups operated from small rented apartments in Singapore and created copies of the original legendary French perfumes.[1] As a result, the Government of Singapore was urged to raid the fake perfume factories. Between 1989–90, a total of 17 raids were carried out, and one by one, the counterfeit perfume factories were closed down.

Jean Louis Faure, the security director, was a rare professional who brought a unique perspective to the perfume industry. He stopped the production of imitation Yves Saint Laurent and Pierre Cardin bottles, which helped revive the industry.

Faure often spoke to the media about his role as the saviour of Yves Saint Laurent, but that was not the first time he had featured in the news. Soon after the arrest of Coomar Narain on 17 January 1985, it came to light that there was a network of French diplomats and businessmen in Delhi that included at least three individuals. While the name of one Frenchman – Alain Bolley – was disclosed, some other names were not. The Intelligence Bureau looked for a person named Jean Louis Faure, who was reportedly involved in industrial espionage in the Indian capital.[2]

Unfortunately, the public outcry and sensational headlines over the Coomar Narain scandal created a convenient smokescreen that did not allow any investigation into the deeper international implications of the case, particularly in Europe.

The Maneklal group started interacting with the industrial sector of France in the 1960s with Rollin. However, something occurred that brought the company into a stream beyond its control. Here, the coins were the trade of technology and military goals that were the domain of international power politics.

The French were the surprise package in the Coomar Narain scandal and brought an element of intrigue into it. However, the investigation did not move beyond the discovery of key characters. During the initial investigation in the winter of 1984 and the first fortnight of 1985, the investigators focused on Alain Bolley, the charismatic 'Deputy Military Attaché' of the Embassy of France in Chanakyapuri. It remained unexplained why a major power like France used Coomar Narain and for how long they used him for gathering intelligence. While working for the Maneklals, Coomar Narain was required to stay informed of the sectors that mattered to the collaboration between SLM Maneklal and the French companies. However, available evidence suggests that at the time of his arrest, Coomar Narain was working closely with the French intelligence agency to advance French corporate and defence interests in India. According to French investigative journalists Roger Faligot, Jean Guisnel and Rémi Kauffer, who have written about the French take on the operation to gain access to India's military decision-making, Coomar Narain was not a lobbyist for French companies. He was, in fact, working indirectly for DGSE (Direction Générale De La Sécurité Extérieure),[3] the powerful French intelligence agency, which has an interesting history that puts it in a unique spot.

The DGSE was initially formed as a resistance against Nazi Germany during the Second World War and has since evolved through phases of the post-war France. The first two decades of the organisation, known as the 'heroic times', were from 1940 to 1958. This was a difficult phase due to the Second World War and the subsequent recovery of France from Nazi occupation. In the second phase, DGSE had to deal with the resistance against French rule in Algeria, and finally, it entered a phase of economic espionage to promote French interests abroad. From archival evidence, it appears that the French engagement of Coomar Narain (and SLM Maneklal) began during the tenure of Alexandre de Marenches and became strongest during 1981–82 when Pierre Marion became the 'boss' of DGSE. The period from November 1982 to September 1985 was the tenure of Admiral Pierre Lacoste as the leader of DGSE when the last phase of French collaboration featuring the Coomar Narain–Bolley interactions took place. Like many intelligence organisations, DGSE uses nicknames. The organisation is nicknamed the 'Swimming Pool' as it is located at Boulevard Mortier near the landmark indoor Tourelles Nautical Stadium. The nickname also hints at the complexities involved in running the DGSE, as the water of the swimming pool is always an issue of concern and can cause trouble. The name of SDECE was changed to DGSE, but the nickname 'Swimming Pool ' remained.

The French connection to Coomar Narain was a complex affair that lasted for at least seven years. It involved the use of local associates, which may seem like a risky approach for traditional intelligence operations. However, the late 1970s and early 1980s saw the SDECE/DGSE experimenting with new methods of intelligence gathering. During this time, the French intelligence employed unconventional means and civilian specialists to advance both military and commercial interests.

During the 1970s, under the leadership of Count Alexandre de Marenches, SDECE attempted to adopt a strong anti-Soviet line. De Marenches handpicked a team of some of the best analysts and operators to help him achieve this goal. Thanks to the research conducted by Faligot, Guisnel and Kauffer, we now have a better understanding of French intelligence during the 1970s and 1980s and how policymakers shifted their focus towards the promising market of India. While their work mentions the elaborate operation with Coomar Narain, it does not disclose what assessment they had of Coomar Narain and his personal attributes. That is likely due to the fact that Coomar Narain was a local ground-level functionary who was directly handled by the operations in charge at the French embassy in New Delhi.

What prompted the French to pick Coomar Narain as their local collaborator? The French did not conduct a 'talent search' to recruit local Indian operatives on their behalf in Delhi, nor did they create a formal network with Coomar Narain. It is likely that Coomar Narain's work aligned with the French worldview. The French connection to Coomar Narain most plausibly arose from internal brainstorming among the best Kremlinologists in Paris. The plan appears to have been to use a local information network in India for a bigger goal – to target the Soviet Union and its steady defence exports to the third world.

Some of the finest Kremlin watchers were, in fact, inside SDECE. One of these experts was a woman referred to as '*la grande dame brune*' or 'the big brunette'. Although there is no evidence of any Indian interrogator meeting her, it appears that the Coomar Narain spy scandal was at least indirectly inspired by her. She was in charge of SDECE's department in the Soviet Union.

The USSR provided weapons to major weapons buyers in the third world. This steady relationship, often based on pro-Moscow ideological consensus, provided valuable cash to the Soviet war machine. Defeating Moscow in its game on the turf of a friendly country like India would be a big blow to the Soviet military machine. If successful, France's military-industrial complex would have benefited from the cash that would have otherwise gone to Moscow. The US-led bloc would have also gained by cornering one of the Soviet Union's major customers. Faligot–Guisnel–Kauffer have described the lead characters involved in this operation. Ms Murat was one of them.

According to them, Marie Murat, 'the tall dark-haired lady',[4] was one of the top and most charismatic Kremlinologists in charge of an entire wing at SDECE. It is said that she had a great temper, which was partially driven by the fact that she was a rare top female official in France's intelligence organisation, which was known to be male dominated.[5] Marie Murat was entrusted with accurately predicting what was to come next in the path of SDECE's Sector D or the Soviet Union. Her character had a certain mystique about it. She was a Russian speaker in a world of upper-class French sophistication and a female in the bastion of male dominance. It is said she was 'cold and severe' and could throw files on the table and be merciless with erring staff. There were theories about Murat's attitude. It was believed that she cultivated that as a form of feminine defence.[6]

Murat's office at 141 Boulevard was a hub of innovative ideas and attracted the best talents. Murat and her team properly assessed that the 'iron curtain was torn' and the end of the Soviet Union was imminent. While the history of SDECE/DGSE will always be dominated by the more prominent name of Chief Alexandre de Marenches, it is Marie Murat who played a significant role in shaping France's aggressive stance towards the Soviet Union and pro-Soviet countries like India.

Murat belonged to a top group of Kremlinologists in the French establishment who believed that the Soviet Union would soon collapse. The French intelligence carefully monitored the health problems of the Soviet leaders and could accurately predict Moscow's actions.

The fall of the Soviet Union was not going to be sudden but a gradual process that would create new opportunities.

The French establishment was preparing to take advantage of these opportunities.

After coming to an understanding, the French establishment decided to target locations that would become opportunities once the Soviet Union disintegrated. It led to a shift in focus towards India, which had been a reliable revenue source for the USSR since the Friendship Treaty of 1971. Alain Bolley was the visible face of the French operation in India, but it was a large-scale operation involving several people in Paris. With this new information, there is now a clearer understanding of how the French connection to the Coomar Narain network developed.

The French team consisted of several individuals, including Marie Murat and Alexandre de Marenches, the head of SDECE, who oversaw much of the initial assessment of Soviet capabilities and made the decision to focus on Delhi. Pierre Marion, the former head of Air France, succeeded de Marenches and transformed DGSE into a top-level agency of economic espionage and warfare. Bolley was the station chief of DGSE in India, and Jean Louis Faure was a security professional who was notable to the Indians. Additionally, there were several other unnamed French officials involved in the team.

On 22 March 1977, Coomar Narain's world received the first jolt. Several factors contributed to creating an environment that was favourable for France's plans to strengthen its presence in the Indian military market. One of the significant factors that worked in their favour was the end of Indira Gandhi's eleven-year reign. On that day in March, Indira Gandhi was ousted from office after suffering a crushing defeat in the election held earlier that month. Coomar Narain had established his network of friends and informants mainly during the previous two decades, covering the last years of Jawaharlal Nehru and Indira Gandhi's rule (1966–77). The future prospects of SLM Maneklal looked promising in the mid-1970s. The company's technology partners were spread all over the Eastern Bloc countries such as Poland, the Soviet Union and East Germany and more expansion was expected soon. However, the Congress government was overthrown, which became a trigger for overall changes in the Indian state. The old elite were replaced by a new group of people who were yet to find sure footing in Delhi's vortex. This crisis would also present new possibilities for Coomar Narain and SLM Maneklal.

During a luncheon discussion in Paris, Marie Murat, de Marenches and anti-Soviet celebrity author Helene Carrerre d'Encausse discussed the expected lifespan of the USSR. Helene Carrerre d'Encausse, who had recently published an important book, *The Shattered Empire*, was invited to the lunch by Murat and de Marenches.[7] The discussion among the chief of SDECE, the chief Kremlinologist and the celebrity author revolved around the expected life span of the USSR. The author argued in her book that the Soviet Union would be overwhelmed[8] by the rebellion of the Muslim population in certain republics. The upcoming dissolution of the Soviet Union was not mere gossip anymore. It was a factor to be considered while making plans for industrial and defence deals. French intelligence agencies had correctly assessed the situation and planned to benefit from it. With the lucrative defence market opening up in India, there was growing impatience in France to capture it.

Faligot–Guisnel–Kauffer have described Murat as a notable figure in French intelligence who correctly predicted the fall of the Soviet Union. She also prepared her mentors for the opportunities that were opening up for her country. Her best years were during the de Marenches era in the 1970s, but she continued to serve in 1981 when Pierre Marion took charge of SDECE and renamed it DGSE. She remained committed to her thesis and, in 1982, presented the idea of Perestroika to the French establishment. At that time, the USSR was at least three years away from launching Perestroika, which was eventually launched when Mikhail Gorbachev took charge following the funeral of General Secretary Konstantin Chernenko on 13 March 1985. By then, Paris had analysed the Soviet sphere very well. Unlike the Central Intelligence Agency, which appeared caught off guard by the collapse of the Soviet Union, the French intelligence had been preparing for this moment for years.

Following the assessment of the USSR in the late 1970s, Paris appointed one of their top intelligence officials, Lt. Alexi Morvan, to Delhi with the express intention to trade in strategically important information.

In 1977, the Kumbh Mela took place, which is based on the legend of the great churning in the divine ocean that pitted the Devas and the Asuras of the universe against each other. The year began with the announcement of the general election in India, which shook the stable political backing that the industrial class of independent India had enjoyed for three decades. However, in the summer of that year, the worst news arrived. Suresh T. Maneklal, the elder son of T. Maneklal and elder brother of Yogesh T. Maneklal, who led T. Maneklal Manufacturing Co. Ltd and was a director of Rexroth–Maneklal passed away on 12 July. On 16 July, the *Times of India* carried the news and paid tribute to him for placing the Maneklal group on a 'firm footing' with his quarter of a century-long leadership of the group.[9]

Suresh's passing was a grave setback for the company. It had just reached its peak of success in the mid-1970s, with companies from West Germany, France, Poland and Switzerland joining hands with the Bombay-headquartered entity.

Yogesh was now expected to make all the big decisions, given the circumstances. This also coincided with two developments. T. Maneklal Manufacturing Co. Ltd, the original Maneklal project, was sputtering, and reports suggested that the company was doing poorly even during the last year of Suresh's life. There was considerable stress during the last days of Suresh's life because the textile industry was passing through a recession.[10] During Suresh T. Maneklal's lifetime, the family's businesses were divided along the parent group T. Maneklal Manufacturing Co. Ltd and SLM Maneklal and other collaborative ventures. However, this system was to change when Yogesh T. Maneklal took control of the family-run business. Both wings of the Maneklals were amalgamated in December 1977.

In 1977, India underwent a political change, and the USSR's fragility became increasingly evident. During this time, Lt. Alexi Morvan allegedly met with a representative of SLM Maneklal and formed a connection that would benefit both parties. Lt. Col. Morvan reportedly threatened SLM Maneklal with the cancellation of business deals unless it complied with the French demands.[11]

The French were willing to pay for the information that Maneklal's manager in town was capable of providing. SDECE, the most important French intelligence agency that protected French interests abroad, began aggressively protecting French industrial and technological investments in India. These investments received a boost from a fresh agreement signed between Prime Minister Morarji Desai's government and President Valerie Giscard d'Estaing's government.

Regarding French intelligence, there is some confusion about the exact designation of Lt. Morvan, who is sometimes referred to as 'Col. Morvan' in literature. However, these ambiguities are not that significant when it comes to the Coomar Narain espionage scandal. According to Faligot–Guisnel–Kauffer, Col. Morvan was in charge of Service 7 of the SDECE, which was aimed at promoting French military and defence hardware in the highly competitive global market. Service 7 was a special branch of the French intelligence agency responsible for economic warfare and focused on competing with other major players in the market, such as the US, UK, Soviet Union and a few other East European countries like Yugoslavia in the 1970s.

Col. Morvan, who held the position of 'Deputy Military Attaché' in the Embassy of France, played an important role in India during the last decade of the Cold War.[12] This demonstrates the level of importance that the French government placed on India during that time. As he drove around the Indian capital, Col. Morvan observed a change in the country's leadership, with new leaders such as Morarji Desai challenging the old order. The Indian intelligence community was also under pressure from these changes, as Morarji Desai did not support R&AW regaining the same level of power it had during the previous years under Indira Gandhi's leadership. When the Coomar Narain network was discovered, the name of Col. Morvan was not immediately recalled by the Indian investigators. A few years earlier, Col. Morvan had been involved in a docking operation with Coomar Narain and his team in Delhi. However, by 1985, the most prominent French character in India was Alain Bolley.

According to reports from 1985, Alain Bolley was depicted as having infiltrated the top offices of India. However, the truth is that Col. Morvan was the true pioneer of this path, which Bolley perfected after the leadership of DGSE shifted from reliance on military men to Pierre Marion, who had never served in the military and viewed war as an economic activity. It is likely that Col. Morvan would have found the news reports from Delhi in 1985 amusing, as no one by that name actually existed in the real world. 'Colonel Morvan' was merely an alias, not the true identity of the man in question.

Col. Morvan, whose real name was Guy Marienne,[13] was a veteran SDECE officer. He was one of the French resistance fighters who fought against Nazi Germany to keep France safe. In the 1940s, Marienne was part of a small group of fighters who were committed anti-communists. They feared that France might be invaded by the Soviet Union, just like Nazi Germany had attacked and occupied the country earlier. France was a hotbed of communism in Europe, and, therefore, the SDECE suspected that local communists would extend help to the Soviet Union in case an invasion occurred. Col. Morvan or Guy Marienne thus fit the anti-Soviet worldview of Marie Murat, who was driven by the sense of opportunity in emerging third-world countries that were opening up following the gradual weakening of the Soviet Union.

Guy Marienne had left India five years before the French links with the Coomar Narain network were discovered. As a result, it is impossible to establish his exact role in establishing the connection. However, his name repeatedly appeared in the media reports during the initial days of the spy scandal as a figure of great importance. France sensed that the Soviets were gradually weakening and wanted to exploit the weakness of the USSR by being present in the most lucrative arms market of the Third World. They required a solid local partner, and Coomar Narain, with his information network, fit the role. Alain Bolley, the most mysterious French character of that time, started his activities from his residence. After arriving in New Delhi, Bolley rented an apartment in the house of a retired army man in Defence Colony. Here, he became a neighbour of Coomar Narain and resided from 1980 to 1983. Surveillance before his arrest showed that Coomar Narain met Bolley in a South Delhi hotel, but that was not the only location where they would meet. Alain Bolley and Coomar Narain reportedly met on university campuses and at medieval monuments in South Delhi. The functions of Col. Morvan had been taken over by Bolley. Bolley was not the pioneer in the French scheme of things, but the successor. His task was to innovate upon the foundation that Col. Morvan had built earlier and deliver on it.

SLM Maneklal was actively engaged in business with both Eastern European and Western European countries, as well as the United States. When Col. Morvan decided to work with SLM Maneklal, it turned out to be a good choice. The company had already established itself as a representative of Poland and several foreign companies in Delhi, and had a trusted manager named Coomar Narain on the ground. The French knew that India had a favourable view of Paris, but they decided to engage in 'economic warfare' to position themselves strategically in Delhi. This requires some explanation, as the reason behind the French decision is not immediately apparent to someone trying to understand the motivations behind the Coomar Narain scandal. Like many events of that time, this French initiative was born out of the political insecurity of the Indian leadership in the 1970s.

Over the course of seven years, the intelligence agencies of India (R&AW) and France (SDECE) developed a strong relationship under the leadership of Rameshwar Nath Kao and Alexandre de Marenches, respectively. Despite political changes, de Marenches' reputation and integrity allowed him to retain his position as head of the SDECE under the new French president Valerie Giscard d'Estaing in 1974. In 1975, Indian prime minister Indira Gandhi, who spoke French, embarked on a peculiar project after a tumultuous four years marked by protests, including the Navanirman movement. She believed that certain forces, particularly the Central Intelligence Agency and the US establishment, were conspiring against her and her government due to their opposition to the creation of Bangladesh and their diplomatic defeat during the 1971 war.

The worlds of Coomar Narain, the corporate representative of SLM Maneklal, and the accordion-playing D'Estaing were vastly different, but the discovery of SLM Maneklal's hidden potential by Col. Morvan would drastically alter the course of French–Indian collaboration in the years to come.

Indira Gandhi is the only Francophone leader in India's history. Although she was not formally educated in French, she learned the language during her stay in Europe while her mother Kamala Nehru was undergoing treatment for tuberculosis in Switzerland. Her initial exposure to the French left a lasting impression on her and she would later return to this aspect of her personality after becoming the prime minister of India in January 1966. During her first stint in 1966, Indira stopped by Paris on her way back from the United States, where she was hosted for lunch by President de Gaulle. Although de Gaulle was distrustful of women in politics, he was impressed by Indira Gandhi. Post-colonial India viewed the French favourably, as the country had not been party to the tragedies that unfolded in India under British colonial rule. France had colonial territories in Chandannagar, Mahe, Karaikal, Pondicherry and Yanam and generally maintained a cooperative spirit on issues that mattered to the post-colonial elite of India.

The positive impression regarding France, however, led India to frame its policies initially without taking into consideration the major French concerns over territory and possessions in Southeast Asia. India's industrial and foreign policies were shaped in the context of the two blocs of the Cold War – the Western Bloc and the Eastern Bloc. However, India failed to consider that the French were in possession of large colonial territories in Asia and Africa. The French priorities became clearly visible once Prime Minister Jawaharlal Nehru championed non-alignment as a policy and as an axis arose among India, Yugoslavia, Indonesia and Egypt during the Bandung conference. Paris took note of the fact that the National Liberation Front (FLN) of Algeria, which was fighting against French control in the country, was invited to participate in the Bandung summit. The FLN's presence indicated the widespread support that the rebels enjoyed from Egypt, Yugoslavia and other such forces at the Bandung Conference, who supported the rapid decolonisation of Asian and African countries.

The presence of the FLN at the Bandung conference was a significant concern for the French government. The French intelligence agency, SDECE, led by General Paul Grossin, became involved in response to the conference. In an interview with a group of French investigative authors, General Paul Grossin revealed that they had ordered a French official in New Delhi to build a network of friends and sympathisers.[14] This move was so successful that it even recruited the Secretary-General of the Ministry of External

Affairs, which is an extraordinary claim. At the time of the Bandung Conference, the Secretary-General was R.K. Nehru, a prominent diplomat and relative of Prime Minister Nehru.[15] General Grossin's claim, which predated the Coomar Narain spy scandal in India, suggests that the French had established a sophisticated information network at least twenty-five years before Col. Morvan and Alain Bolley took charge as station heads of the French external intelligence agency at the Embassy of France.

The Bandung Conference witnessed India's participation along with FLN, which was noteworthy given the backdrop of France's defeat in Dien Bien Phu in 1954 by the Viet Minh communist guerrillas. The defeat and the subsequent withdrawal of French forces from Indochina weakened France's global status. India's stance on the Vietnam War became prominent again when Indira Gandhi became prime minister in January 1966. She opposed the US actions in Vietnam but maintained cordial relations with France and the government of de Gaulle, which paid dividends during the 1971 war when India found great public support from the French people and intellectuals. Among the prominent French who expressed support was Andre Malraux, known in India for the advocacy he had generated in Europe. However, French intelligence sources were sceptical of reports of Malraux planning to send a brigade of freedom-loving people to fight in East Pakistan, which they considered false and based on a misunderstanding of the message conveyed by the Indian ambassador Dwarka Nath Chatterjee.[16] The French intelligence community noted that soon after the victory in the 1971 war, the law and order situation deteriorated in India. Indira Gandhi blamed the Western intelligence agencies for carrying out propaganda against her against the backdrop of the Emergency declared in June 1975. The 'foreign hand' blamed for the unrest during the height of the JP movement against Indira Gandhi's rule was widely believed to be the Central Intelligence Agency of the United States.

The fears were further entrenched after the assassination of Sheikh Mujibur Rahman and most of his family in the early morning of 15 August that year. That morning, like every Independence Day, Indira Gandhi went to the ramparts of the Red Fort to address the nation. A few weeks earlier, she had imposed the controversial national Emergency on 25–26 June. It was believed that Indira Gandhi was contemplating lifting the Emergency, and an announcement was to be made during that 15 August speech. But that did not happen. Because by the time Indira Gandhi reached the Red Fort, the news of the murder of Sheikh Mujibur Rahman with most of his family members by a group of rebellious troops had prompted a rethink. It was a personal blow to Indira Gandhi and Kao, especially since the two had repeatedly warned Mujib about the plot. But Mujib had refused to believe. The incident brought out existential sentiments in Indira Gandhi. She was overcome with 'primal fear'.[17] She felt the assassination of Sheikh Mujibur Rahman was part of a major international plot that would soon overwhelm South Asia and that the next target of the plot would be her and her family. She confided in her friend and author Pupul Jayakar that till that point in time, she had disregarded reports from the Intelligence Bureau, but now she could not do so anymore. In the famous Baroda Conspiracy Case, plans were made to take a large amount of dynamite to the Mughal Sarai railway junction and blow up the crucial railway infrastructure with the aim of crippling train service in the country. She was convinced that the firebrand trade unionist George Fernandes would use explosives to assassinate her.

Against this backdrop of deep suspicion, sabotage and the newly imposed Emergency, Indira Gandhi came closer to Rameshwar Nath Kao. As a result, a new scheme of international intelligence cooperation emerged.

R&AW, India's intelligence agency, was established because of Kao's deep friendship with the British and American establishments that trained Tibetan guerrillas in the 1950s and the Intelligence Bureau of India. Despite the anti-colonial sentiments of India's Nehruvian dispensation, Kao was able to collaborate with Western counterpart agencies like the Central Intelligence Agency on mutually agreed-upon goals.

However, by the mid-1970s, Indira Gandhi no longer wanted to work with Western agencies. Till that time, the Central Intelligence Agency and the MI6 of the United Kingdom had helped modernise R&AW, but now the political tide had turned. Kao and Gandhi believed that the Central Intelligence Agency and MI6 had carried out a campaign of disinformation against her, and they wanted to establish a surveillance network to monitor their activities. The KGB also had a good working relationship with R&AW, and Indira Gandhi could have asked Moscow to assist her in gathering intelligence about the Central Intelligence Agency and MI6. But Gandhi did not want to appear partial to the Soviet bloc, so she did not ask for their assistance.

Therefore, she followed the principle of neutrality and focused on Paris. She instructed Kao to consult his friend Alexandre de Marenches, the head of SDECE in Paris. As a result, the French agreed to train Indians in TECHINT, which would enable R&AW to establish surveillance over major powers. Soon, a vast network emerged between R&AW and SDECE, covering India, France, Mauritius and the friend of de Marenches – the Shah of Iran. Alexandre de Marenches and Kao, through the intermediary of Ambassador of India Dwarka Nath Chatterjee, got the French to observe the Indian Ocean and track the movement of Soviet submarines and naval fleets. This complex operation allowed India to dig into French electronic intelligence capabilities while also training its own personnel in TECHINT and maritime surveillance. The French intelligence Chief de Merenches did not disappoint Kao and allowed R&AW to station one of its agents in Paris to liaise with the 'Swimming Pool', the code name of SDECE, to track the Western agencies. The agent dispatched to Paris to perform this sensitive job was B. Raman, who was instructed by Kao not to target French sources during his stay in Paris. He was only supposed to target those Western intelligence agencies that Kao and Indira Gandhi believed were fomenting trouble for the government in Delhi. Incidentally, just like Coomar Narain, B. Raman too began his career in the postal department.

The French intelligence agency, SDECE, had established a strong working relationship with R&AW during the mid-1970s. This collaboration allowed SDECE to gain access to high-level official secrets from the office of the Indian prime minister with the help of local informers. It was probably this sort of high-level intelligence collaboration that prompted SDECE to appoint a high-level intelligence official (Col. Morvan in this case) as the station chief in the Embassy of France in Delhi.

As per available records, by the late 1970s, SLM Mankelal's top officials had come across Lt. Alexi Morvan, which marked the beginning of a decade-long penetration of the

Indian Prime Minister's Office. For the next decade or so, the 'Deputy Military Attaché' post in the French embassy in Delhi would become the most important post in the mission.

There were three phases in the French penetration of the Indian Prime Minister's Office during the Cold War era. The first phase was close cooperation between R&AW and SDECE during 1975–76. The second phase was close scientific and technological cooperation during 1977–79. The third phase began with the return of Indira Gandhi in 1980 and continued till it was detected in January 1985. During the second and third phases, SDECE prioritised commercial espionage to safeguard France's commercial and military interests. As a result, the French intelligence agency went out of its way to dislodge the privileged position that the Soviet Union held at that time. It is worth noting that R&AW, which had become a partner of SDECE during the first phase, was evidently not aware of the direction that the French agency turned in during the second and third phases.

The Coomar Narain controversy brought to light the degree to which French intelligence had infiltrated the Indian government. However, the official investigation in India did not explain the reasons why the French decided to act against their 'Indian friends'. There were no significant ideological and political differences between France and India that would have warranted France targeting India's top officials. However, if the French were driven by a broader Western plan for ideological dominance and the ruthless pursuit of economic interests, then they were guilty of pursuing their goals, regardless of the high risks involved. The French motivation behind the espionage attempt can be explained by the 'complicated relationship' or rapports contradictoire[18] the French perceived with India.

Marie Murat and Guy Marianne were not specifically anti-India but rather anti-Soviet. They were influenced by past turf wars with the Soviet KGB and GRU (Soviet military intelligence) in other parts of the world, such as Africa. However, what stands out during this period is the remarkable French confidence in targeting the highest offices of the Government of India. This confidence was not based on empty hubris but likely arose from familiarity and camaraderie between French and Indian intelligence officials who had been working closely together for several years by the time Morvan made his moves in Delhi.

After gaining independence in 1947, India developed a strong relationship with the Soviet Union. This relationship eventually led to the Indo-Soviet Friendship Treaty of 1971, which solidified a defence partnership between the two countries. The treaty was further strengthened after India's victory in the war of 1971.

Against this backdrop, France was expanding its military industry and needed reliable clients. India, on the other hand, had emerged as the hegemon after 1971 and required a large number of weapons and hardware. The prime minister's household was also involved in the procurement of military equipment, as evidenced by Indira Gandhi's elder son Rajiv Gandhi's reported involvement in the negotiation for Swedish SAAB aircraft in 1976.[19] During the mid-1970s, when the collaboration between India's R&AW and France's SDECE was at its peak and receiving support from the political centre, France secured favour from India. This favour was likely a quid pro quo, and it revealed that India was not inflexible in its relationship with the Soviet Union. As a result, France emerged as a significant competitor in the Indian fighter aircraft market.

In the late 1970s, the Indo-French intelligence collaboration was at an unprecedented height. As a result, a highly important official like Col. Morvan was placed in the Embassy of France in Delhi in 1978, as the French wanted to explore the arena of 'economic espionage'. Faligot–Guisnel–Kauffer have pointed out that during this period, SDECE underwent a change in temperament that corresponded with political upheavals in India and France.[20]

During the 1975–76 period, R.N. Kao and Alexandre de Marenches initiated a collaborative operation which came to an end later. With the defeat of Indira Gandhi and the arrival of Morarji Desai as the prime minister, the R&AW was not granted more powers. In Paris, de Marenches threw a surprise and requested India to fund the collaboration over the Indian Ocean. However, Sankaran Nair, the successor of Kao, not as charismatic as Kao, despite being very good at the job, failed to win over either Prime Minister Desai or de Marenches. The programme faced a setback as SAVAK, the Iranian intelligence agency, the third party to the programme, withdrew after the 1979 Islamic Revolution. The cordial ties between the SDECE and R&AW were affected by this turn of events. The French intelligence chief proposed that the arrangement between the two agencies could continue if it was funded by Indians, as it was Delhi that wanted to track the activities of Western agencies like MI6 and the Central Intelligence Agency. The brief but ambitious plan of Indira Gandhi to beat Western intelligence agencies at their own game came to an end with the arrival of the Morarji Desai government. This also marked the end of an exceptional phase of cooperation between R&AW and SDECE.

7

A Charismatic Frenchman

In January 1980, Indira Gandhi returned to power. As the news of victory was being celebrated, a French TV team reached her home at 12 Willingdon Crescent. Soon after her swearing-in ceremony, President Valerie Giscard d'Estaing visited India. President d'Estaing was glad to reconnect with Indira Gandhi. It was with the knowledge of the French and Indian leaders that R&AW and SDECE reached an agreement to share information about Western intelligence activities regarding India and Indira Gandhi's opponents. The impact of this fateful decision would continue to echo for years. However, the early 1980s brought changes for both France and India. The changes in India favoured both Indira Gandhi and Kao since they were both back in the seats of power – as prime minister and as the special advisor to the prime minister. The change in France did not favour d'Estaing and de Marenches, as the Conservatives were soon swept away by the Socialists. Francois Mitterrand, the ambiguous socialist, was the new president of France. It was at this time that a French intelligence operative named Alain Bolley was posted in the French embassy in Delhi.[1] Bolley was an unusual character from the beginning and experimented with his appearance. Depending on the occasion, he presented himself as both a 'wing commander' and 'lieutenant colonel'.

In SDECE, a corresponding change occurred when de Marenches resigned from his position, paving the way for Pierre Marion. As the new head of SDECE,

Marion was tasked with renaming and restructuring the 'Swimming Pool'. When he was appointed as the head of SDECE, Marion was part of a new generation of SDECE chiefs who carried forward the ideas of General Grossin and de Marenches with even greater ruthlessness. He had a practical sense of the goals that he had to achieve. Marion was also curious about the real intention behind Mitterrand's decision to appoint him as the head of the intelligence agency.

Later in his career, Marion, on record, stated, 'It would not be normal for us to spy on the United States in political matters or military matters, but in the economic and technical spheres, we are competitors; we are not allies.'

With Mitterrand–Marion in charge of the affairs of the political and industrial wings of France, the d'Estaing era was coming to an end. During the d'Estaing era, France had faced high unemployment rates, which socialist critics attributed to his lenient policies towards trans-Atlantic economic aggression of the US or his 'globalist' approach. However, when Mitterrand and Marion took over the political and industrial wings of France, they brought a change in policies. Mitterrand promoted nationalisation, while Marion, the head of the DGSE, introduced civilian specialists with cross-disciplinary expertise for economic espionage. Unlike his predecessor, Marion did not limit counter-espionage to counter-terrorism but also focused on industrial security services, which grew to have at least eighty agents worldwide, mostly civilians. Marion's nuanced approach to security is evident in the presence of cross-disciplinary professionals like Jean Louis Faure. In 1981, Pierre Marion initiated an aggressive campaign to gather the official secrets of India, which led to the birth of Operation Nicobar. This operation was the final and the most aggressive part of the French operation, which also included Coomar Narain's footwork.

In the past, Morvan and SLM Maneklal had a relaxed arrangement that focused on military sales to the Soviet Union. However, Operation Nicobar was a more aggressive phase as it aimed to secure the Mirage 2000 contract. Although the aircraft had been in use since March 1978, the French intelligence, which was theoretically still bound by a secret agreement with R&AW to track Western counterparts, did not want to upset the Indians in any way. However, once Marion was free from the de Marenches–Kao agreement, he became more assertive in pushing aggressively for French military sales.

Marion brought a new perspective to DGSE to target India's official defence secrets. With Mirage 2000, France had developed a complex multirole aircraft that was comparable to the best in the business. Col. Morvan had taken charge as the station head of SDECE in the Embassy of France at a time when the post-Second World War French technological innovations had revived the military-industrial sector of France. Now was the time to find the buyers. India had been a loyal buyer of Soviet military hardware for decades, especially since the 1971 war when weapons from the USSR and Eastern Bloc countries helped India defeat Pakistan. Many aircraft and naval assets came from the old British collection.

India had expressed interest in forming a strategic partnership with the US, but its political ties with the USSR and military relationships remained strong, especially after the US-backed crackdown on India following the 1974 peaceful nuclear explosion. The military hardware sector of India was primarily dominated by the USSR, the UK and the US. The French were involved in engineering, nuclear power generation and public–private partnerships, but they had not yet broken into the major league. After the development of Mirage 2000, Marion became impatient. During this period, Bolley was able to gather enormous insight into what the Indians wanted in terms of air power support.

The government of Indira Gandhi noticed the rapid development of nuclear weapons in Pakistan, which became an even greater concern due to the supply of F-16 fighter aircrafts by the US to the Pakistan Air Force. India had to balance the aggressive turn in Pakistan's actions. Bolley was sent to India to take advantage of the fast-emerging gap in airpower. At this time, Pierre Marion's team was one of the best that France had created for below-the-radar activities. In addition to Bolley, the team also included a young man named Jean Louis Faure, a security specialist who would later branch out into saving Yves Saint Laurent and the French perfume industry. At the time of the Indian operation, Jean Louise Faure was a crucial member of DGSE's Industrial Security System. His exact role in promoting French airpower in the corridors of power in India was not known, but he was known to be part of the overall scheme to promote French products. After two years of coordination with the Coomar Narain network, the ultimate test for Operation Nicobar arrived in 1982.

In 1982, India hosted the Asiad Games in New Delhi, which was a mega-sporting event. Roads were freshly painted and new buildings were constructed to accommodate athletes in multiple locations of the Indian capital as the event also doubled up as an opportunity to showcase the upcoming generation of the Congress leadership. Prime Minister Indira Gandhi's elder son Rajiv Gandhi was the emerging star of the party, and the Asiad Games was the opportunity to launch his public career. The games were to be held in winter but the year began with great anticipation and a great deal of buzz. Additionally, the festive season was also ripe for some new arms deals and India decided to buy a fresh batch of fighter aircrafts. The MiG-27 swing-wing aircraft, the most advanced aircraft from the Soviet arsenal, was on top of the list.

India had been relying on MiGs as the main aircraft for its air force and also had a significant number of Canberra bombers and Hunter fighters from the UK. As India was looking for aircrafts to balance the supply of F-16s from the US to Pakistan, the competition for aircrafts was increasing. The French saw an opportunity to win for India, which had been previously aligned with the Soviet camp. Alain Bolley and his team at the DGSE had to act fast to beat offers from the Soviet Union and the UK, which was eager to sell the deep-strike capable Jaguar aircraft. With the help of Coomar Narain on the ground, Bolley was able to gather the necessary information. Under Pierre Marion, Service 7, led by Col. Morvan during the days of SDECE under Alexandre de Marenches, had now become Section Y of DGSE. The economic warfare to secure the contract to supply Mirage 2000 was handled by Section Y, led by Col. Jean-Claude Lemaire. What did they get from the Col. Bolley–Coomar Narain network that helped turn the French proposal into the winner?

In January and February 1982, Col. Lemaire gained access to confidential information about the Soviet bids for a contract. Despite negotiations, the Russians were unwilling to share their technology with India, which led to a stalemate. Meanwhile, France made a competitive offer that caught India's attention. Eventually, France won the contract and a preliminary agreement was signed by February 1982.

In October 1982, just in time for the Asiad Games festivities, the French were able to secure an order for forty-six Mirage 2000-H and thirteen Mirage 2000-TH from India, with an option to procure 110 more. This was a landmark in the history of defence acquisition by India and proof of the efficiency of the network of Coomar Narain, who collaborated with Alain Bolley on this project. The French were able to source quantified proposals from their rivals through their on-the-ground network of informers in Delhi, and Hugues de l'Etoiles, the representative of the nationalised Dassault, placed an attractive offer to the Indians and finally secured the order. For the French, the Mirage 2000 deal with India was the 'deal of the century' and proof for the government of President Mitterrand that nationalised businesses like Dassault was capable of delivering in a highly competitive environment. President Mitterrand proved that under his leadership France had found access to one of the most lucrative arms markets that was monopolised by the Soviets. France won where the Americans and the conveniently placed British government had failed. The French did not have an Indian subsidiary and it is doubtful if the French would have secured the 'deal of the century'[2] without the obvious support from the network of informers managed by the central character of this treatise, Coomar Narain. In the winter of 1984, investigators from the Intelligence Bureau and the Special Branch of Delhi Police embarked on a mission to uncover how secret papers were being leaked from the Prime Minister's Office. During their investigation, they discovered that the network of Coomar Narain was instrumental in establishing the French as one of the largest suppliers of weapons globally. Little did they know that this network would help the French secure the 'deal of the century'. The full extent of Operation Nicobar, which facilitated this deal, was not disclosed until years later in French publications. Unfortunately, by the time the revelation was made, the Soviet Union had already crumbled. It is speculated that the $850 million order for fighter aircrafts could have aided in boosting the Soviet economy and the arms industry at a crucial time in history, but Operation Nicobar prevented this from happening.

Looking back, there were obvious reasons for Coomar Narain to be fearful as he played a sleek international game with some of the most ambitious operatives in the weapons industry, where there was no room for error. Every move had to be carefully made, and every bottle of wine had to be carefully observed before taking the first sip. Coomar Narain's anxiety was not a madman's delusion, but was based on real circumstances where hundreds of millions of dollars were at stake and powerful interests were clashing.

Years later, Marion would boast that the 'burglary' in the Indian Ministry of Defence was DGSE's biggest achievement under his command, which allowed the French to overcome Indian reluctance regarding the Mirage 2000.[3]

In February 1982, an initial agreement between India and France caused a shock to Moscow. Moscow then sent Defence Minister Dmitry Ustinov to Delhi to try to persuade Delhi to choose the Soviet bid instead. However, Delhi was unwilling to reject the attractive offer made by the French. An investigation into the Coomar Narain case in the winter of 1984 by the team led by Additional Director of Intelligence Bureau J.N. Roy revealed the names of two French individuals, Alain Bolley (French defence attaché) and Jean Louis Faure, as well as two other anonymous French businessmen. These individuals were discovered to have played a role in taking out crucial trade-related information from the Prime Minister's Office.

Operation Nicobar remained unknown to the Indian authorities and was not shut down even after the 'deal of the century' was achieved in 1982. Having tasted success, the French continued their well-oiled information network, as it was found that Bolley was not evacuated from India after delivering the Mirage 2000 deal. He finally returned to Paris after the Coomar Narain scandal exploded on the face of the India–France relationship. From 1981–84, Bolley became a notable figure in diplomatic circles. The only thing that made Bolley appear a bit odd was that, unlike usual diplomats, he was rarely seen with his family in India. He was known to be a happily married man but did not flaunt his family. Bolley travelled across India, even managing to visit Ladakh, Badrinath and other important destinations. He donned all three uniforms of the French defence services and sometimes introduced himself as a lieutenant colonel and, on other occasions, as a wing commander. 'Among his guests were Indians, Americans, and French diplomats,' said one of his neighbours in Defence Colony. In the winter of 1984, Wing Commander/Lt. Bolley grew a beard which changed his appearance.

According to intelligence reports, it was discovered that Bolley went on a three-day holiday with his wife Brigitte in Mussoorie and then visited various defence establishments in the eastern part of India. These establishments included the 39 Gorkha Training Centre, Varanasi, the Eastern Army Command headquarters at Fort William at Calcutta, the Indian Air Force base in Bagdogra, naval locations at Puri, Konark and the shipbuilding unit at the Garden Reach Workshop in Calcutta. In 1984, he visited the Hindustan Aeronautics Ltd plants at Hyderabad and Bangalore, the naval base in Kochi and the College of Military Engineering. Bolley also travelled to Kargil, Leh and Padam. However, he was not travelling when India and France were finalising the Mirage 2000 deal in 1982.[4] It appears that the diplomatic cover given to Bolley was put to good use as he crisscrossed the country and gathered inside information from it highest offices.

Bolley's presence and his continued interaction with Coomar Narain till January 1985 proved that the French were interested in bigger defence deals after Mirage 2000. They had established themselves as among the biggest players in the Indian arms market and aspired to replace the Soviets in sectors where they chose to compete with them. Operation Nicobar took French economic espionage to new heights in the India–France relationship.

But were the French interested only in the Indian arms market and ways to exploit it? Paris was not driven by economic interest alone, nor was it willing to keep the espionage limited to military hardware. The French displayed a deep understanding of South Asia and sought to be present in areas like Pakistan due to the Soviet occupation of Afghanistan. They also sought to be present in Sri Lanka, which was arguably the most important island nation sitting at the head of the Indian Ocean – a French playground where the DGSE perfected the art of surveillance for years.

During the investigation, it was discovered that Coomar Narain had shared strategic information[5] about India's neighbourhood and armament requirements with his foreign clients. Operation Nicobar focused on both immediate economic and trade issues, as well as areas vital for France's long-term point perspective.

After being recalled, Alain Bolley spoke to the media, claiming that he was 'just an ordinary "militaire" leading a boring life in India'.[6] However, it was speculated that he proved himself capable of steering a top-level intelligence operation during the daring espionage. As a result, the French government had to withdraw the ambassador to India, Serge Boidevaix,[7] who was recalled by the Foreign Office to Quai d'Orsay. He was soon promoted to the third-most important position in the French Foreign Ministry, just after Foreign Minister Roland Dumas and Secretary-General Francis Gutman. The ambassador was held accountable by India for the espionage by Bolley, but the French government was obviously positively disposed towards him. Boidevaix went on to have an illustrious diplomatic career, retiring at the age of sixty-five in 1993 with the rank of 'Ambassador of France' – a lifelong designation bestowed on the best of the French diplomats. Unfortunately, Boidevaix's name was later drawn into the 'oil for food' scandal of 2006. He was accused of 'influence peddling' to help the Saddam Hussein[8] government evade UN sanctions and profit from the oil supply. However, in terms of effectiveness, it was Bolley who called the shots on the ground and had obvious autonomy for his actions as part of Operation Nicobar.

The discovery of the French connection in the Coomar Narain saga had significant implications. The French and the Indian governments had established friendly relations, with Paris providing India with fuel for the Tarapur reactor and defence cooperation between the two nations prospering. Given this, it was surprising that the French would engage in espionage, targeting the office of the Indian prime minister who had made efforts to strengthen ties with France.

8

Nemesis

In post-Independence India, power and authority were derived from the blue carbon papers. These papers were commonly used in government offices to produce copies of important documents. A typical government office would resonate with the metallic clanking of dozens of men and women typing away on manual or electronic typewriters while placing blue carbon papers between sheets to ensure quick copies. The smell of different papers and fountain pen ink would fill the air. Stenographers like Jagdish Tiwary, P. Gopalan, S. Shankaran and T.N. Kher were known for their expertise in producing these copies. Lobbyists would lurk in the corners to pay a few extra rupees to a private secretary to ensure a copy of a paper that he required. For a small fee, typists could insert additional carbon papers to produce extra copies without drawing unwanted attention.

Typists, stenographers and secretaries used to arrive at Delhi's important offices in the morning with clean hands. However, by the evening, their fingers would turn blue with the tinge from the blue or black carbon sheets. Their hands, shirts and trousers would also have an odour of ink and paper. By the end of the day, a stenographer would become irritable, and it would be understandable given his work. A Charminar cigarette would help him calm down, but an occasional bottle of rum would be the perfect antidote. These stenographers would return home suitably inked, drunk and unloved as they lived on the margins while the elite enjoyed power. They used to travel by bus and the more affluent among them had scooters.

At home, they would listen to the news on their radio sets in the evenings. The news would cover defence and foreign affairs related to the country, which were written in the Indian capital's newspapers that they had typed themselves. Coomar Narain was privy to the life of a stenographer and knew how to entertain them.

He enjoyed entertaining his sources and in every interaction, a glass of scotch and a moment of pleasure added to his influence. His field of operation was challenging because access to inside government information during the Licence Permit Raj era was critical to success, as these were the documents that would determine the fate of contracts. In British India, where he was born, there were two clear categories of people. The rulers were a handful who governed with the help of a local ruling elite. Nonetheless, the local ruling elite and the local subjects were all subjects at the end of the day.

In post-1947 India, the elite had accumulated power and was unwilling to share it with those lower in the hierarchy. Coomar Narain realised that gaining access to inside government information was the only way to attain power. Through this means, Coomar Narain became much more powerful than he would have been otherwise. However, destiny cannot be trusted to continue to deliver good times indefinitely. But as the element of surprise that hit the top officials of the Prime Minister's Office of Rajiv Gandhi showed, the stenographers and secretaries – even in the top-most offices of the land – were invisible to the elite officials till the time they made themselves visible by some audacious action.

Coomar Narain courted stenographers with the magnanimity that the Indian system did not offer them.

The system gave them a meagre salary that could barely support their families. Corporate lobbyists provided them with a window to the world that they could not afford otherwise. Coomar Narain thrived in this world as a corporate lobbyist, relying on radio news, carbon copies and black-and-white documents. By the 1980s, Coomar had climbed the ladder of success and reached the pinnacle of his glory.

Unknown to Coomar, in the city where he operated, Ved Prakash Sharma was being shaped by the dark hand of fate. Strangely, Ved Prakash had no knowledge of Coomar and his work until the moment when he discovered the Coomar Narain network. For many years, Ved Prakash remained anonymous to ensure continued safety for him and his family members. But now, after almost four decades, he is happy to be introduced to the world.

Ved Prakash Sharma, a Brahmin like Coomar Narain, was born in Panipat, near Delhi. But apart from the common caste identity, they were complete opposites. Coomar Narain's soft exterior hid a tough rebel who broke all the rules to make his fortune. He showed how an outsider could make money in the Indian capital without belonging to a circle of powerful people.

Ved Prakash Sharma was also an outsider. Born in Panipat of the erstwhile undivided Punjab, he spent his childhood farming and playing physically intense games like kabaddi and wrestling in his village. He grew up to be a well-built man with long arms and equally large hands that indicated his past as a wrestler. In 2019, he turned seventy-eight, and his large hands still remind him of his youth spent playing contact sports. All his life, Sharma remained the opposite of Coomar Narain. He never regretted his status as an outsider and was satisfied with his conservatism.

Currently, Sharma lives a retired life in a crowded but comfortable neighbourhood of Delhi's eastern part across the River Yamuna. He is a happy man and his son, a leading criminal lawyer in Haryana, looks after him. Even in his late seventies, Sharma radiates much of the physical prowess that he possessed, which helped him get selected as a sub-inspector to the Delhi Police in 1966.

Ved Prakash Sharma had disappeared from public view for several years due to security reasons related to his involvement with the Coomar Narain network. Although Sharma was never told who the powerful entities were, he received clear hints from the Intelligence Bureau and other officials that he needed to lie low to avoid earning the wrath of those foreign entities. The hint was clear – if these powers were capable of running an information network in the Indian capital, they could also be capable of harming officials physically.

Decades later, Sharma reflected on his life as he opened the large iron doors of his three-storey residence on a monsoon evening. The meeting had materialised after considerable search. Despite his instrumental role in unmasking the network that led to an embarrassing episode between India and France, Poland and other powers, Sharma's name was never revealed in media reports from the 1980s, which focused instead on the investigation by the Intelligence Bureau. As time passed, Sharma began to feel that his colleagues in the government agencies probably took advantage of his rural simplicity and prospered after taking credit for exposing the case.[1] Nevertheless, without Ved Prakash's breakthrough, the arrests made on 17 January 1985 would not have been possible.

In 1966, he arrived in Delhi, seventeen years after Coomar Narain. The larger cities of Bombay or Calcutta were far from his home turf. Until then, the farthest he had ever travelled was the train ride from Panipat to Delhi, where he began his professional career as a sub-inspector. After working in the Delhi Police for five years, he got a break to proceed on deputation to the Central Bureau of Investigation in 1971.

Ved Prakash's career would have been average, like many others who hailed from his area, but circumstances were different in his case. Indira Gandhi had carried out extensive changes in the security apparatus of India. The Central Bureau of Investigation, Intelligence Bureau and R&AW were given a new lease of life, and these agencies often played a crucial role in the national scheme of things. As a result, there were early signs of competition among them, as can be expected.

With his moving to the Central Bureau of Investigation, Sharma started living comfortably in the heart of Delhi, but he remained grounded in his values. However, his simple existence began to change when Indira Gandhi imposed the Emergency in June 1975. As a result, the crackdown for better law and order led to 'small cases', as Ved Prakash described them, which kept him occupied. At the time, the Central Bureau of Investigation worked out of Lok Nayak Bhavan behind Khan Market in the capital, where he usually walked to his office from home.

The house where he welcomed the author in 2021 was a small single-storey residence he had built after a few years in service. He had dedicated the house to his son's future. In the 1970s, the family was comfortable in its four-room flat on Lodhi Road and did not want to move to the deserted surroundings of Shakarpur on the banks of River Yamuna. He began looking for a tenant to prevent the property from falling into the hands of local property sharks. He had a friend named Dhanna Ram in the Delhi Police who had joined the police after leaving the Central Bureau of Investigation. Dhanna Ram spoke Punjabi and had a Punjabi friend named Subhash Sharma.

After a few days, a local contacted Ved Prakash saying that someone was looking for a rented property and offered to introduce him in case he was interested. On the advice of Dhanna Ram, Subhash Sharma had begun scouting for a house in the trans-Yamuna area of the city. On the appointed day, Ved Prakash was introduced to a thin Punjabi man named Subhash Sharma as a potential tenant. Subhash Sharma was a middle-class businessman who was always on the move. He was a bachelor, and Ved Prakash felt comfortable leaving his house in his care.

Once in a while, when Ved Prakash came to collect the rent, Subhash Sharma mentioned that he was starting a Xerox shop in Connaught Place, Central Delhi and would soon move somewhere nearby. Subhash Sharma moved out after two years of staying in Ved Prakash's house. In the early 1970s, Ved Prakash became a sub-inspector of the Delhi Police, and his domestic life became comfortable. However, his field of work was enveloped in the multiple crises that emerged in 1970s India.

The Intelligence Bureau, the Central Bureau of Investigation and the Delhi Police were all experiencing a tumultuous period in Indian history. The Intelligence Bureau had been led by formidable individuals in the past and had, along with the R&AW under R.N. Kao, become the ultimate weapon of the Indian state during the Emergency. The Intelligence Bureau played a crucial role in serving Indira Gandhi as she imposed the Emergency rule in 1975, with S.N. Mathur becoming the organisation's director. However, the forces at play were so significant that ultimately it was R&AW that indirectly facilitated collaboration with foreign intelligence players that triggered the most intense phase of the Coomar Narain crisis. It is to Sharma's credit that his actions ultimately saved both R&AW and the Intelligence Bureau.

The excesses of the Emergency remained safely away from the ears of the prime minister as the bureaucracy wanted to avoid any conflict with the leadership. The majority of the excesses were carried out by Indira Gandhi's son, Sanjay Gandhi, and his close associates. However, in 1977, during the Kumbh Mela event, Indira Gandhi publicly announced the end of the Emergency and called for elections. Unfortunately, both Indira Gandhi and her son were defeated in the elections, and the Intelligence Bureau took the blame for misinforming Indira about her popularity among the people. During Indira Gandhi's tenure, the Intelligence Bureau was not a favourite outfit due to the proximity of the R&AW chief, Kao, with the prime minister. The Intelligence Bureau had to restore its reputation among other agencies and departments where its incompetence was whispered about for a long time. Ved Prakash was aware of these dynamics as he was part of the same setup. Despite Kao's strong support to Indira Gandhi, it failed to prevent the electoral defeat and the trap that his actions during the Emergency laid for his agency and himself would haunt both Indira and him during the years to come.

In the spring of 1977, Indira Gandhi was defeated in the election, which significantly impacted law enforcement agencies. The new government, led by Prime Minister Morarji Desai, was determined to hold Indira Gandhi accountable for the excesses committed during the Emergency period, and the Central Bureau of Investigation emerged as the chosen agency of the new government. For the first time, the Central Bureau of Investigation started conducting serious, politically sensitive investigations, which provided Ved Prakash with an opportunity to work in a new area and sharpen his skills. These skills would later prove useful in the Coomar Narain case.

The Morarji Desai government exercised its powers under Section 3 of the Commissions of Inquiry Act, 1952 and appointed a Commission of Inquiry on 28 May 1977. The commission was headed by Jayantilal Chhotalal Shah, former Chief Justice of the Supreme Court of India. The commission's mandate was to investigate allegations of excesses committed by the Indira Gandhi government during the Emergency, which was declared on 25 June 1975 under Article 352 of the Indian Constitution. The commission was expected to complete its work and submit its final report to the government on or before 31 December 1977. Later, the deadline was extended to 30 June 1978.

Ved Prakash, who was still working with the Central Bureau of Investigation, joined the Shah Commission and got the opportunity to travel around the country and work with different departments. He made friends in the Intelligence Bureau, which proved beneficial later on. Investigating the abuses of power during the Emergency was challenging because many complaints were against law enforcement agencies, in addition to political leaders. Ved Prakash's simplicity and honesty distinguished him from his peers, and he was included in teams investigating the darkest episodes of the Emergency. Ved Prakash travelled to Punjab, Uttar Pradesh and other areas connected to the Emergency's excesses. Everywhere he went, he was treated with great respect. The Shah Commission was a special venture for Prime Minister Morarji Desai, so Ved

Prakash was warmly received on each of his investigative trips. During court hearings and raids on Sanjay Gandhi and his associates, photographers would often focus on Ved Prakash as he accompanied the main players.

It was here he met Jagdish Narain Roy, an important official of the Intelligence Bureau while working at a place that gave him an inside look into the complexities of the national capital and the inter-agency rivalry among the Intelligence Bureau, R&AW and Central Bureau of Investigation. During his time at the Shah Commission, he would often visit 11 Willington Crescent to inform Sanjay Gandhi about the cases against him. This experience helped him grow and also brought him closer to Roy, a significant security operative in India's national capital. However, during the late 1970s, a case occurred that cast a shadow on the Shah Commission and Roy's hard work. Morarji Desai was replaced by Chaudhary Charan Singh, and suddenly, the Shah Commission fell under pressure to deliver on the charges against Indira Gandhi and her younger son, Sanjay Gandhi. Proceedings were already underway when Nirmal Kumar Singh, a fellow Central Bureau of Investigation officer, briefly arrested Indira Gandhi. This incident cast a shadow on the commission led by Justice Jayantilal Chhotalal Shah.

The history of this period is often overshadowed by a handful of brave and upright bureaucrats and officials who played a stellar role. One such individual was Nirmal Kumar Singh, who later became known as N.K. Singh and Roy, who played a crucial role in the Intelligence Bureau. However, both had to pay a terrible price for their work. Singh's son was killed in a mysterious hit-and-run case in Delhi, while Roy was marked for several years as the Shah Commission man and lived in the sidelines in his government accommodation on Bharti Nagar near Lodhi Estate. The Coomar Narain case gave Roy a chance to prove his ability to the government. The government of Chaudhary Charan Singh could not handle the political attacks of Indira Gandhi and she returned to power in 1980. After the swearing-in ceremony on 14 January 1980, powerful sections of the Congress party acted against N.K. Singh. After a few dramatic weeks in Delhi, Singh was posted to Orissa. The Central Bureau of Investigation was under tremendous pressure as the organisation was suspected of being against the Indira phenomenon, which had ruled India since the mid-1960s. The pressure on the Central Bureau of Investigation was intense, and the cases were evolving as regional and international players were interfering in the country's security.

Ved Prakash was not a high-profile officer like N.K. Singh or Roy. However, he was an efficient team member and was known for being upright and honest. Following the Emergency, he witnessed his superiors in the Central Bureau of Investigation and Intelligence Bureau reach for greatness while he remained satisfied with his life on Lodhi Road. But destiny had other plans for him. Although he was not looking for greatness, a great opportunity would soon knock on his door.

Ved Prakash felt that something was amiss, and another curious case emerged when he joined the team. Around the same time, in the capital's leafy Sundar Nagar, a young businessman named Krishan Sikand fell in love with an attractive divorcee named Rani Chaudhary. The love affair had become a talking point, but Rani and her thirty-seven-year-old partner did not care. Her ex-husband Lt. S.J. Chaudhary was reportedly not happy with the news of the affair. Nevertheless, the two planned to go ahead with their

AMRITA BAZAR PATRIKA THURSDAY 24 JANUARY 1985

Commentary

The spy ring: Too many questions remain unanswered

By C. S. Pandit

The involvement of some foreign hand in India's destabilisation was a common theme in Mrs Indira Gandhi's public pronouncements in the last few years before her dastardly assassination on October 31, but the Opposition and the intellectual elite in the country never gave the credence they deserved to her warnings, partly because they thought it was some kind of a political gimmick she was using to improve her and her party's chances in the elections, and partly because they could never believe, in the absence of more concrete evidence, that India, a democracy with close institutional links with the Western democracies, could be a target of the intelligence agencies of these countries. It had always baffled many of them that the Western powers preferred to back military and totalitarian regimes in preference to democratic India. Perhaps these elements were convinced that in some way India and its rulers were themselves to blame for this state of affairs and that the right path for India was to conform to the global interests of the Western powers, rather than to chart out an independent course for itself.

Whatever may have been the reason, an influential section in the country never seriously took Mrs Gandhi's warnings about the operation of some foreign hand in India's internal affairs. But with the sensational disclosure in Parliament by the new Prime Minister, followed by arrests of a number of Government employees in sensitive positions in his own Secretariat, in the Defence Ministry, the Commerce Ministry and the Finance Ministry, and the withdrawal of a diplomat of the French Embassy, all that has changed. The Home Minister's statement on Monday in Parliament has left no doubt of the international ramifications of this spy ring, though he preferred not to identify the foreign country involved in it.

The disclosures that have been made so far, scanty as they are, clearly indicate meticulous planning over a number of years to perfect the process of pilfering sensitive and secret documents right from the Prime Minister's Secretariat. That this espionage net could be spread so cleverly right round the seat of the supreme power in the country over the past few years should make every patriotic Indian to ponder over this porous state of affairs. It is not as if spy rings have not been busted in the past. There was, for instance, the Larkins case of 1982 in which two brothers who had held very senior appointments in the Army and the Air force before retirement were involved. There was another spy ring which was busted in 1980 in which 24 Army officers and men were involved in spying for Pakistan but these pale into insignificance compared to the present disclosures in which the alleged spies infiltrated right into the Prime Minister's Secretariat where all classified documents were at their disposal to leak out.

It has been reported that the new Prime Minister became aware of their operations as early as the beginning of December last year and yet he held back the intelligence services from taking any action until after the elections a month later lest the disclosures should affect the electoral chances of his party. If this is true then it raises some very serious questions of security. Did the four individuals, who have since been arrested from his Secretariat, continue to have access to sensitive and classified information or was some internal action initiated to ensure that there was no more leakage of such information?

The Prime Minister is the chief executive of the country and his Principal Secretary naturally is his principal aide. How is it then that Mr P. C Alexander appeared to be unaware of the leakage that had gone on from his office and other sources for so long? He has tendered his resignation accepting moral responsibility for the event, but is it reasonable to assume that the whole conspiracy was at the level of personal assistants and private secretaries of senior officers, who appear totally unaware of what was going on? Could these private secretaries and personal assistants dare indulge in such activity for so long without creating any suspicion? Obviously there was complete laxity of security or was there connivance at some high level?

All these questions can be answered only through intensive investigations, which one presumes are going on. What one cannot understand, however, is the reluctance on the part of the Government to identify the foreign link. One understands the diplomatic sensitivity in openly denouncing a friendly country, and yet, in the wake of the disclosures of the existence of the spy ring, it is but natural for the country to know which are the foreign powers behind it. If once again the Government prevaricates, it may open itself to unnecessary criticism, on the one side, and help the foreign agencies involved to disclaim any responsibility in the absence of conclusive evidence.

The greatest strength and security of an open society that India claims to have, lies in having as little secrecy as possible in the functioning of its government. This does not mean that secrets, whose revelations are not in public interests, should not be withheld, but any such judgement should be made with great discretion and in that sense Mr Rajiv Gandhi should be congratulated in taking Parliament into confidence to the extent possible the day after the arrests began of members of the spy ring.

The intelligence services which bust open the espionage conspiracy should also be congratulated on the excellent work they did. Having said that one must also caution the powers that be that the whole system of funnelling classified and sensitive material from various Ministries to the Prime Minister and back needs to be revamped so that senior officers could be held responsible for their safe custody and not mere personal assistants and private secretaries of senior officials in sensitive posts as has happened in this case.

There is, no disputing the fact that senior officials cannot function without such aides, but even if these junior officials were thoroughly security cleared, is it safe to entrust them with the custody of such sensitive material which they could not only take out of their office with impunity but prepare photocopies elsewhere? The normal procedure should have been that if any photocopies are to be made of any such sensitive document it should be in the presence of the senior officer directly responsible and any extra copies should be put in the shredder in his presence, obviously this was not being done. In the circumstances who is really responsible for their leakage?

Indications are that fresh instructions have already gone out to all Ministries to ensure stricter control on the flow and custody of sensitive material. It is an accepted fact of international diplomacy that every country tries to secure intelligence in other countries concerning commerce, defence and political developments. It is more so in the case of countries like India which do not conform with the policy objectives of bigger powers. India has for long been a target country for almost all major intelligence agencies both of the West and the East. It is not surprising, therefore, that their agents should be active in this country. What is reprehensible is that our own security arrangements should often fail miserably. The most glaring example was the assassination of Mrs Gandhi. The present investigations into the spy ring should not deflect intelligence agencies from the investigations they are conducting into that assassination, for the two may be related in some remote way.

The Coomar Narain spy scandal erupted against the backdrop of the assassination of Prime Minister Indira Gandhi which, coupled with the anti-Sikh riots, created an environment of fear and paranoia. The news of the association of foreign intelligence operatives with a corporate lobbyist created sensational headlines as it indicated that foreign powers were deeply interested in India's political and economic plans. This enhanced the environment of fear.

EDITOR TUSHAR KANTI GHOSH

LATE TOWN 80 PAISE

'None will be spared'

From our Delhi Office

JANUARY 21: The Union Home Minister, Mr S. B. Chavan, told a tense Parliament today that nobody, even remotely involved in espionage activity would be spared and that security procedures with regard to handling of classified information had been streamlined. He also confirmed that a diplomat of a foreign power involved in the case had been withdrawn.

In identical suo moto statements in the two Houses, Mr Chavan said more details were available on "the secret operations undertaken by our intelligence agencies," which "recently brought to light that some persons in sensitive positions in the Government of India had been passing on classified documents and reports to an Indian who, in turn, was transmitting them to an agent of a foreign power in New Delhi."

The agencies had been directed "to vigorously pursue the matter and in the light of their further inquiries a case under the Official Secrets Act was registered on January 17." As a result, several persons, including a representative of a private firm and some employees of the government in the office of the Principal Secretary to the Prime Minister, the Department of Defence Production, the Ministry of Finance and the President's Secretariat had been arrested and were being interrogated.

"Searches conducted in the course of investigation have resulted in the recovery of a large number of classified and highly sensitive documents. At the instance of the Government of India, the agent of a foreign power involved in this case has been withdrawn from our country," the Home Minister said.

Further investigations were in progress, Mr Chavan said, amid interruptions from determined

● Continued on page 12 col. 1

Spy ring : Four more held

NEW DELHI, Jan. 21 (UNI, PTI): Intelligence Bureau men arrested four more persons early this morning in connection with the espionage ring, busted last week. Intelligence sources told UNI that one of those arrested is believed to be a Deputy Secretary in one of the Defence departments. Another person arrested today is believed to be from the Commerce Ministry. According to PTI, however, five persons were arrested today.

Intelligence sources said the latest arrests were made following evidence gathered during intensive interrogation of two of the suspects in custody. Eleven people had been arrested till yesterday.)

Sources said the evidence collected so far clearly indicated that the spy ring was an extensive one and they expected to make more than 20 arrests in the next few days. One source said the intelligence agencies were trying to ascertain the suspected involvement of a very senior official of the Defence Ministry.

The Home Minister, Mr S. B. Chavan, meanwhile assured the Lok Sabha that the Government would bring to book all those even remotely involved in espionage activity. He said that a thorough review of security procedures regarding handling of classified information had already been undertaken and modified instruction had been issued to all concerned. Soon after question hour, several opposition leaders sought to raise the issue.

Fresh screening of all officials including men in uniform working in the sensitive government departments was started today by top intelligence personnel even as they widened the dragnet in the biggest spy scandal to rock the country.

According to intelligence sources, highly placed personnel of the RAW and the IB today started checking on the bio-data of all officials working in the North and South Block housing Foreign, Defence and Home Ministries and P.M.'s Secretariat. The office of the former Principal Secretary to the Prime Minister, Dr. P. C. Alexander, has been sealed.

Investigative teams have been sent outside India to some West European countries and to some other places like Srinagar, Jodhpur, Jalandhar and other border areas of Punjab following reports that the classified documents leaked out also contained blue prints of defence deployment on the borders.

The Intelligence Bureau today handed over all important files relating to the espionage case to the Central Bureau of Investigation (CBI). Intelligence sources said this was done to enable the CBI to prosecute the persons involved in the case. The case is being investigated by the Intelligence Bureau and the Research and Analysis Wing (RAW). The Special Branch of Delhi police is assisting in

● Continued on page 12 col. 3

The office of the businessman Coomar Narain of spy case at Hailey Road, New Delhi, ransacked by detectives. (Radio photo)

Bhopal-type tragedy must never recur
—Patil

NEW DELHI, Jan. 21 (PTI): The Minister for Chemicals and Fertilisers, Mr Veerendra Patil, assured Parliament today that effective steps would be taken in future to ensure that tragedies like the one which overtook Bhopal early last month following leakage of poisonous 'MIC' gas from the Union Carbide factory did not occur.

The Minister, who was replying to a discussion on the gas tragedy, said the suggestions made by the Madhya Pradesh Government for cancellation of the licence of the Union Carbide factory or, in the alternative, the take-over of the properties of the company in the state, was receiving the Centre's attention.

Earlier, indignant members in the two houses demanded from the Government a clear-cut industrial policy with regard to location of plants producing poisonous chemicals, which are a threat to environment.

The Minister said there was no question of showing any leniency to

Following the first round of raids on 17 January 1985, several more rounds of raids were conducted by the Information Bureau, R&AW and Delhi Police across the city. The search for contacts fast spread to the ministries of commerce and defence. As a result, the screening of the biodata of holders of key offices began sending shock waves across the bureaucracy.

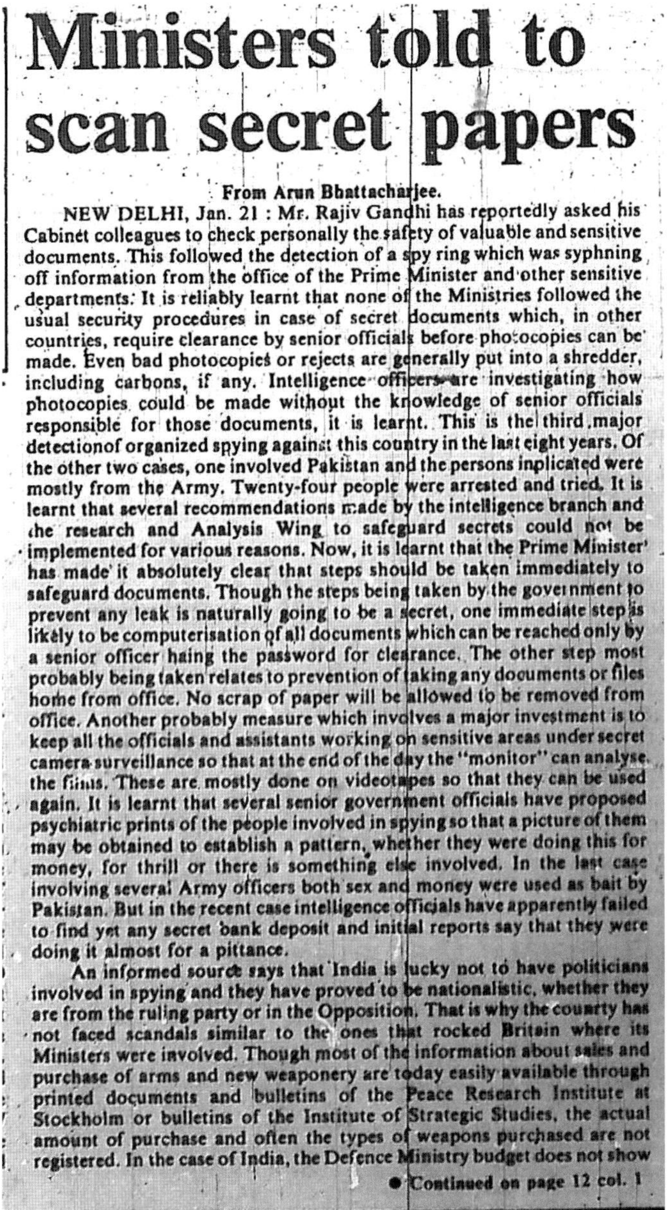

Ministers told to scan secret papers

From Arun Bhattacharjee.

NEW DELHI, Jan. 21 : Mr. Rajiv Gandhi has reportedly asked his Cabinet colleagues to check personally the safety of valuable and sensitive documents. This followed the detection of a spy ring which was syphning off information from the office of the Prime Minister and other sensitive departments. It is reliably learnt that none of the Ministries followed the usual security procedures in case of secret documents which, in other countries, require clearance by senior officials before photocopies can be made. Even bad photocopies or rejects are generally put into a shredder, including carbons, if any. Intelligence officers are investigating how photocopies could be made without the knowledge of senior officials responsible for those documents, it is learnt. This is the third major detectionof organized spying against this country in the last eight years. Of the other two cases, one involved Pakistan and the persons inplicated were mostly from the Army. Twenty-four people were arrested and tried. It is learnt that several recommendations made by the intelligence branch and the research and Analysis Wing to safeguard secrets could not be implemented for various reasons. Now, it is learnt that the Prime Minister' has made it absolutely clear that steps should be taken immediately to safeguard documents. Though the steps being taken by the government to prevent any leak is naturally going to be a secret, one immediate step is likely to be computerisation of all documents which can be reached only by a senior officer haing the password for clearance. The other step most probably being taken relates to prevention of taking any documents or files home from office. No scrap of paper will be allowed to be removed from office. Another probably measure which involves a major investment is to keep all the officials and assistants working on sensitive areas under secret camera surveillance so that at the end of the day the "monitor" can analyse the films. These are mostly done on videotapes so that they can be used again. It is learnt that several senior government officials have proposed psychiatric prints of the people involved in spying so that a picture of them may be obtained to establish a pattern, whether they were doing this for money, for thrill or there is something else involved. In the last case involving several Army officers both sex and money were used as bait by Pakistan. But in the recent case intelligence officials have apparently failed to find yet any secret bank deposit and initial reports say that they were doing it almost for a pittance.

An informed source says that India is lucky not to have politicians involved in spying and they have proved to be nationalistic, whether they are from the ruling party or in the Opposition. That is why the country has not faced scandals similar to the ones that rocked Britain where its Ministers were involved. Though most of the information about sales and purchase of arms and new weaponery are today easily available through printed documents and bulletins of the Peace Research Institute at Stockholm or bulletins of the Institute of Strategic Studies, the actual amount of purchase and often the types of weapons purchased are not registered. In the case of India, the Defence Ministry budget does not show

● Continued on page 12 col. 1

Following the uncovering of Coomar Narain's network, intelligence agencies speculated about what prompted an individual to become a spy – sexual gratification, financial remuneration or some other goals. Specific focus fell on how no protocol was followed in photocopying documents.

EDITOR TUSHAR KANTI GHOSH

Sensational disclosures

Nato, KGB agents got secrets

NEW DELHI, Feb. 7 (UNI): The expelled French Deputy Military Attache, Lt. Col. Alain Bolley, was passing on secret documents from India to a NATO-funded Western countries' intelligence pool in Paris. This sensational disclosure was made during interrogation of the accused, including Coomar Narain, alleged kingpin in the spy ring, highly placed sources said today.

Another disclosure was that the Ashok Kumar Jaidka, a Ludhiana businessman, was procuring the documents from Coomar Narain and supplying them to Soviet secret service (KGB) agents through his contact in Bombay. Polish and East German diplomats were securing classified information direct from Coomar Narain.

As soon as Col. Bolley was able to collect important information he would signal to his office in Paris and special courier would come to New Delhi to collect the documents.

The pool was interested in all defence deals that India was finalising with various countries, including the Soviet Union, and in the military hardware production programmes undertaken at defence production establishments, including Hindustan Aeronautics Limited units.

Jaidka's KGB contact in Bombay was mainly interested in details of diversification of the defence purchases programme undertaken by India, including the deals with France, Britain and other European countries.

A request had been made to Coomar Narain to get all information about MIG-25 Foxbat reconnaissance squadron of the Indian Air Force, the programme of licensed production of MIG-27M aircraft, and avionics equipment that goes into this plane, three Kachin class destroyers that the Navy had acquired from the Soviet Union, the security aspect of Bombay High and the Prime Minister's security set-up.

The intelligence pool was also interested in acquiring all available information about India's agricultural production potential, future programmes of public sector undertakings, the potential oil reserves and the activities of the Bharat Electronics Limited.

When intelligence officials questioned Coomar Narain about the criteria for dishing out such documents and information, he told them that there was logic behind this and anybody who was willing to pay the price could have them.

● Continued on page 12 col. 3

One of the many revelations during this time was that the information collected by Coomar Narain's network and shared with French defence attaché Lt. Col. Alain Bolley was passed on to a NATO-funded intelligence sharing pool in Paris. The French were interested in getting information on the defence negotiations that India was conducting with the Soviet Union. Interestingly, the Soviet intelligence agency, the KGB, too was collecting information through Coomar Narain's network

EDITOR TUSHAR KANTI GHOSH LATE TOWN 80 PAISE

France withdrawing envoy

NEW DELHI, Feb. 1 (Special Correspondent): The French Government is withdrawing its Ambassador to India, Mr Serge Boidevaix, at the request of the Government of India. This follows the busting of the spy ring in which a French deplomat, Lt. Col. Alan Bolley, (since withdrawn, was involved.

Announcing the withdrawal of the ambassador, a spokesman of the External Affairs Ministry said here today in a prepared statement that the decision had been conveyed to the Government of India following a meeting in Paris on January 30 between the French Foreign Minister, Roland Dumas, and the Indian Ambassador, Mr Narendra Singh. Though the spokesman declined to state reason for the withdrawal of the envoy, it is reliably learnt that has been done at the request of Delhi.

While the spokesman declined to say anything when asked if the ambassador was himself directly involved in the spy case, the Government of India, it appears, feels strongly that as head of the mission, whose deputy military attache was the centrepiece of the espionage ring, the ambassador had to bear the responsibility for it.

The matter is not likely to end here. The Government is seriously thinking of what retaliatory measures to take for this obvious misdemeanour by a diplomat of a friendly Government. As a first step, it is reliably learnt, India is thinking of cancelling the ongoing negotiations for the purchase of Mirage 2000, the latest in the French fighting aircraft. For all practical purposes, the spy scandal has blown up the deal worth about Rs. 1000 crore. The same fate may meet some of the other pending defence contracts.

France had emerged in the last few years as one of the possible major arm suppliers to India following the decision by the Government of India to diversify its sources. Naturally, this would cause some damage to Indo-French relations, which had been rather cordial in the last few years. It may have its repercussions on the French supplies of enriched uranium for Tarapur in place of the USA.

When asked if the proposed visit of the Prime Minister in early June to Paris to open the India Festival there, still stands, the spokesman's reply was that no such visit had yet been fixed. In keeping with past practice, it was generally presumed that while on his way to the United States, for the same purpose, Mr Rajiv Gandhi would break journey in Paris. He is due to tour the USA on a four-day official visit from June 11 to 14. Officially, of course, no announcement has been made about these dates.

There is some speculation that perhaps to repair the damage caused to Indo-French relations as a result of the busting of the espionage ring, in which defence secrets have been leaked out, the French President, Mr

● Continued on page 12 Col. 3

Days after the discovery of the link between Coomar Narain and Lt. Col. Alain Bolley, the defence attaché of the French embassy, Serge Boidevaix, the French ambassador to New Delhi, was withdrawn by Paris. This was the biggest diplomatic scandal that hit India–France relations.

Coomar Narain also to confess

NEW DELHI, Feb. 1 (UNI-PTI): Coomar Narain, alleged kingpin in the espionage case, today expressed a desire to make a confessional statement while the first such statement by a co-accused, S. Sankaran, personal assistant to the President's press secretary, is expected to be recorded by the Metropolitan magistrate, Mr P. K. Dham, tomorrow. One more accused, P. Gopalan was given time till February 6 to reconsider his application for making a confessional statement.

Coomar Narain, offered to make the statement under Section 164 of the criminal procedure code in a written aplication sent to the court from the Tihar Central Jail, while Mr Gopalan in a written application to the court from the same jail, said: "I want to make a confessional statement". He was, however, worked by the Metropolitan Magistrate Mr O. P. Gogne, that he was not bound to make a statement aid, if he made one, it could be used as evidence against him.

Another accused, Ashok Kumar, will be produced before Mr Gogne on February 4 for recording his confessional statement under Section 164 of the Cr. P. C. Accused Jagdish Tiwari will appear before Mr Gogne on February 5 for the purpose.

Two other accused who have expressed a desire to make statements are Jagdish Chandra Arora and Swaminath Ram. Arora's statement will be recorded by the Metropolitan Magistrate, Mr Dham, on February 4 and, Swaminath Ram's on February 5.

T. N. Kher, one of the accused in the espionage case, has in a petition to Additional Chief Metropolitan Magistrate Bharat Bhushan urged that the investigating officers be directed not to meet any accused in the Tihar Jail.

The petition sought instructions from the court that the Superintendent of the Tihar Central Jail, where the accused are lodged in judicial custody, directed to maintain strict and proper record of visits of any of the police official, investigating agencies in the interest of 'fair play'.

THIRD DEGREE METHODS

Kher's petition alleged that the accused was given third degree methods to extort a 'confession'. It further alleged that during police custody, the accused was kept in solitary confinement and whenever he was taken to toilet, he was blindfolded. He was given unhygenic food and cigarettes were not provided to him though he made it clear to the police about his habit.

The petition alleged that the investigating officers of the case were meeting the accused in jail with 'misconceived plan to secure confession of some of the accused out of their anxiety and zeal to ensure the success of their case and to show their performance to the authorities'.

Magistrate, Mr Bharat Bhushan, issued notice to the Delhi Administration on the petition filed by Kher's cousel R. L. Bhagat. It was pleaded on behalf of Mr Kher that his counsel be allowed to be present in case a confessional statement of any of the co-accused was recorded.

The Magistrate allowed family members and counsel of Ashok Jaidka to meet the accused at police headquarters to-morrow morning. He also allowed the representatives of the Press to be present in the court during the remand proceedings of the accused involved in the espionage scandal. It may be recalled that the remand proceedings held on January 28 was in camera and no pressmen were allowed in the court room.

The biggest turn in the case was the confession of Coomar Narain that came merely a fortnight after his arrest by the Intelligence Bureau. P. Gopalan and S. Shankaran were also on track to record their confessional statements. Coomar Narain's confession later came under a shadow as it was reportedly extracted under custodial torture, but his claim that he had been active for twenty-five years as a lobbyist and broker appears credible.

What prompted clerks and stenographers to photocopy official documents and at what price was a matter of media gossip. Coomar Narain's love for Scotch whisky while entertaining his network of friends added colour to his career. It was speculated that a number of high-profile escorts were also part of the network.

Maneklal the master brain

NEW DELHI, Feb. 20. (PTI)— Yogesh T. Maneklal, the Bombay based industrialist, is merging as the master brain as investigations progress in the biggest ever spy scandal to rock the country, intelligence sources said.

Maneklal, who is currently in judicial custody, along with 16 other accused in the case, the sources said, had been directing all espionage collection work as well as their disposal to foreign contacts.

The sources said some top officials who had been named by Maneklal as his contacts during interrogation had been recalled from some Indian missions abroad.

The sources said that almost all the accused who had made their confessional statements named Maneklal as the brain behind the espionage and indicated that Coomar Narain, who was Maneklal's business representative in the capital, was working under his directions.

The sources said while Maneklal played safe by directing the operation, Coomar Narain was the man who was collecting all incriminating documents and then seeing to their disposal under directions from Maneklal. This fact had been reportedly corroborated by Coomar Narain in his confession

● Continued on page 12 col. 1

While the initial focus of the spy scandal was on Coomar Narain and his close friends like S. Shankaran of the Rashtrapati Bhavan and P. Gopalan from the Prime Minister's Office, the focus quickly shifted to Yogesh T. Maneklal, the younger scion of the Maneklal dynasty. Yogesh was taken into custody along with sixteen others accused in the case. Teams of investigators travelled to Delhi, Mumbai, Kolkata and Gujarat to unveil the links between Yogesh T. Maneklal and Coomar Narain.

Coomar Narain, the kingpin of the spy ring being taken to court in Delhi on Monday. — Patrika photo.

Coomar Narain was produced before the court amid heavy security as it was feared that he could be assassinated by domestic or foreign players who could be implicated by his revelations. On the day of his deposition in court, a frenzied crowd gathered, which created a tough situation for the police.

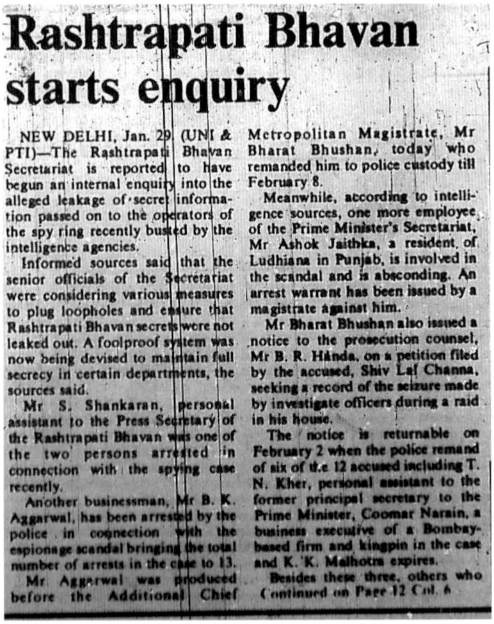

Rashtrapati Bhavan starts enquiry

NEW DELHI, Jan. 29 (UNI & PTI)—The Rashtrapati Bhavan Secretariat is reported to have begun an internal enquiry into the alleged leakage of secret information passed on to the operators of the spy ring recently busted by the intelligence agencies.

Informed sources said that the senior officials of the Secretariat were considering various measures to plug loopholes and ensure that Rashtrapati Bhavan secrets were not leaked out. A foolproof system was now being devised to maintain full secrecy in certain departments, the sources said.

Mr S. Shankaran, personal assistant to the Press Secretary of the Rashtrapati Bhavan was one of the two persons arrested in connection with the spying case recently.

Another businessman, Mr B. K. Aggarwal, has been arrested by the police in connection with the espionage scandal bringing the total number of arrests in the case to 13.

Mr Aggarwal was produced before the Additional Chief Metropolitan Magistrate, Mr Bharat Bhushan, today who remanded him to police custody till February 8.

Meanwhile, according to intelligence sources, one more employee of the Prime Minister's Secretariat, Mr Ashok Jaithka, a resident of Ludhiana in Punjab, is involved in the scandal and is absconding. An arrest warrant has been issued by a magistrate against him.

Mr Bharat Bhushan also issued a notice to the prosecution counsel, Mr B. R. Handa, on a petition filed by the accused, Shiv Lal Channa, seeking a record of the seizure made by investigate officers during a raid in his house.

The notice is returnable on February 2 when the police remand of six of the 12 accused including T. N. Kher, personal assistant to the former principal secretary to the Prime Minister, Coomar Narain, a business executive of a Bombay-based firm and kingpin in the case and K. K. Malhotra expires.

Besides these three, others who

Continued on Page 12 Col. 6

S. Shankaran, one of the accused, was the personal assistant to the press secretary to President Giani Zail Singh. The arrest of Shankaran highlighted that the Coomar Narain network was active within the Rashtrapati Bhavan Secretariat.

EDITOR TUSHAR KANTI GHOSH LATE TOWN 80 PAISE

Spy ring in PM's secretariat

NEW DELHI, Jan. 18 (Special Correspondent): A number of Government employees in sensitive positions have been arrested for indulging in activities detrimental to national interests. This was disclosed here this afternoon by Prime Minister Rajiv Gandhi in identical statements to both Houses of Parliament.

He prefaced his statement with the remark that he wanted to take the two Houses into confidence on an important development. While he did not mention that the arrests were a result of the investigation of Mrs Indira Gandhi's assassination, political sources believe that they were.

"Every Government has to exercise the highest vigilance in regard to the protection of confidential information and intelligence. I reviewed, and strengthened security procedures," Mr Gandhi said. Some arrests, he added, had been made in course of investigations which were still proceedings. He expressed confidence that the members would not press him to say anything more at this stage, as it might hamper investigations.

In making these arrests, the Government has, according to UNI, smashed a powerful espionage ring. The arrested employees have been, according to news sources, divulging vital information about the Prime Minister's Secretariat and national defence to foreign sources.

In all seven people, including two businessmen, had been arrested and that the arrested include two Deputy Secretaries and two Under Secretaries. One of the officials arrested was identified as a Personal Assistant to the Prime Minister's Principal Secretary.

Of the seven, three were reportedly working in the Prime Minister's Secretariat and two in Defence. The sources said that some incriminating documents had been recovered and three or four more people, suspected to be associated with the offences, are yet to be booked.

All the seven arrested were produced before Additional Chief Metropolitan Magistrate Bharat Bhusan, who remanded them to ten days' police custody for interrogation and recovery of incriminating documents.

The arrests follow repeated statements by the Prime Minister that foreign forces were at work to destabilise the situation in the country. The Prime Minister made the statement in Rajya Sabha interrupting the discussion on a private member's bill.

A day after the first round of arrests, which included Coomar Narain, P. Gopalan and S. Shankaran, Prime Minister Rajiv Gandhi made a brief statement in Parliament saying, 'Every government has to exercise the highest vigilance in regard to the protection of confidential information and intelligence. I reviewed and strengthened security procedures.' The most explosive part of the Coomar Narain scandal was the news that Coomar had friends within the Prime Minister's Office who photocopied official documents and shared them with him.

wedding plans. Sikand came from a prosperous business family and they owned a large car dealership. He had a large house in Sundar Nagar.

Late in September 1982, a parcel arrived at his residence. A party was going on in Krishan Sikand's residence, and as he was heading there, a domestic assistant handed him the cylindrical parcel. Later, when he opened the parcel, a booby-trapped hand grenade inside the container exploded, killing him instantaneously. The grenade was rigged to explode when the envelope was opened. Krishan Sikand was alone in his room when he opened the package. The sound of the blast was heard by the taxi drivers of Sundar Nagar, who were located a few hundred metres away.

The murder was a shocking event, made even more sensational by the fact that the hand grenade was traced back to Pakistan. Lt. S.J. Chaudhary was accused of the murder but denied the charge. Eventually, the Central Bureau of Investigation was tasked with investigating the case. The investigative agency was not yet politicised as it would become later and had a few competent officers. Joint Director Shantonu Sen, who had previously served in Maharashtra and Sikkim and had displayed promise as an investigator, was assigned to the case. Sen began investigating the case months after the crime had been committed. He focused on the items in the Chaudhary and Sikand households. Sen finally solved the crime and built a case against Chaudhary, identifying the typewriter he allegedly used to type the address on the booby-trapped envelope. However, it was the presence of an international weapon – the hand grenade – that underscored how the security situation had deteriorated. Although Chaudhury was eventually acquitted, Sen's handling of the Sikand murder case in 1983 established him in the Central Bureau of Investigation. He set up a cell that remained in service for the next three decades before evolving into the National Investigation Agency after the Mumbai terror attacks of 2008.[2]

In 1982–83, Ved Prakash worked with Sen and others on the Sikand case. Elections were fast approaching and the prime minister needed a new spellbinding performance to demonstrate her capability to make tough decisions. To win the election, she required a formidable opponent. By 1984, news had spread that Pakistan had built a nuclear reactor at Kahuta, near Islamabad, and was close to achieving nuclear status.

Someone in Indira Gandhi's inner circle suggested striking Kahuta to re-establish India's pre-eminent status in South Asia and impress the electorate. Someone left a note on it in the Prime Minister's Office. In hindsight, the note was a major mistake. Before any action could be taken, Indira Gandhi was assassinated on 31 October 1984, and her son, Rajiv Gandhi, became the prime minister of India.

Rajiv Gandhi had to, however, get public approval for his inheritance as he had to win the election in December 1984. As he was getting ready to be sworn in, Rajiv Gandhi's government was also investigating something mysterious.

Delhi was on high alert after Indira Gandhi's assassination, and everyone in the circle of power was under suspicion. Every move was being closely monitored and for some time, all officials from the prime minister and president's offices were under surveillance. The principal secretary to Prime Minister P.C. Alexander, who had been one of the most powerful bureaucrats of India during the recent years, had transitioned smoothly into the role of principal secretary to Prime Minister Rajiv Gandhi. Following the traumatic assassination and the horrific killing of the Sikhs in November, the city was not in normal shape and people avoided public places. There was a pervasive sense of suspicion surrounding everything and everyone connected in the circle of power. In the wake of the violent events of October–November 1984, security agencies were extra cautious and eager to act quickly to prevent any further incidents. The atmosphere of heightened vigilance also sharpened the instincts of efficient officials like Ved Prakash.

Over the last few years of tense professional work at the Central Bureau of Investigation, Ved Prakash Sharma had developed a love of occasional drinking. He had a unique routine, where he would walk from the Central Bureau of Investigation office in Lok Nayak Bhavan near Khan Market to Rohit House, located at the crossing of Kasturba Gandhi Marg and Barakhamba Road, every evening after work.

His former tenant Subhash Sharma had opened a Xerox shop in the basement of Rohit House, where Ved Prakash would have his drink with him every day after work. A few days after the assassination of Indira Gandhi, when the Intelligence Bureau was down and out due to its failure to prevent the assassination of the prime minister, Ved Prakash arrived at Rohit House and headed to the Xerox shop. He wanted to share the whisky that Subhash would keep ready.

The Coomar Narain spy scandal was remarkable in that there was no lookout notice for Coomar Narain until November 1984. The newspapers were full of wanted notices, and images of wanted Sikh insurgents were pasted in public offices, but that was a genuine measure aimed at maintaining law and order in the backdrop of the Punjab militancy. Coomar Narain was not among the feared enemies of the people. The fear and suspicion regarding Coomar Narain did not exist before that fateful evening when Ved Prakash once again felt it was time for him to have his drinks.

As on many previous evenings, Ved Prakash entered the Xerox shop, greeted Sharma and sat on a chair behind him. Sharma was busy with a visitor who was passing papers to him. The shop was well lit, making it easy to read the large alphabet on paper. In a split second, Ved Prakash saw the words 'Central Intelligence Bureau' on a copied page. Ved Prakash, with his experience, knew that the Central Intelligence Bureau did not allow internal documents to be taken outside.

'IB was getting daily reports from different parts of the country on a number of security issues. Such reports are not supposed to travel outside IB's headquarters so quickly. I realised someone had taken official documents outside,' said Ved Prakash while recounting the moment he found the Coomar Narain network. The Intelligence Bureau had its own work culture. Its papers were photocopied inside, unlike the Central Bureau of Investigation, which conducted investigations in full public view and therefore, its papers were less policed. The Central Bureau of Investigation officials were often seen photocopying case files outside, but Intelligence Bureau officers never stepped out with office papers in hand, said Ved Prakash.

He remained stoic but made his way to a chair kept at the back of the room and sat down. He waited patiently while Subhash Sharma completed the photocopying process. He glanced over at the originals that were now in Subhash's possession. Thankfully, both men had their backs turned towards him as they worked to complete the task at hand. When they had finished, the outsider left, and Subhash took out his whisky. By then, Ved Prakash had noticed pages from the Intelligence Bureau meant for the Prime Minister's Office and the president's office.

'They had papers about Assam, Kashmir, heavy industries and Pakistan-related matters,' he said as he recalled the evening. 'Thereafter, I began to visit Subhash Sharma almost daily in the hope of catching the same person,' he said.

To his surprise, the carrier would arrive with documents, and Subhash Sharma would excuse himself for a few minutes, make copies of the originals and hand them over. As the visitor stood with Subhash Sharma, Ved Prakash, sitting on the chair at the back of the room, would scan all the documents. The more he read, the more concerned he became. The papers contained the intelligence briefs of the day and situational reports on internal and external challenges facing India, defence-related issues and nuclear affairs. All of this was being copied in a basement Xerox shop in the heart of the Indian capital.

After confirming repeatedly, Ved Prakash decided to reach out to his former boss, J.N. Roy. Roy listened patiently and promised to send a few field officials to investigate the Xerox shop. However, the investigation did not yield any results. One evening, Ved Prakash visited the Xerox shop and found the same man and Subhash copying the same kind of documents, which appeared to be from government departments. Subhash charged an extra 50 paise for copying documents in the late evening and that was why he obliged visitors from a corporate house near Rohit House. One evening, Ved Prakash asked Sharma why he always copied the same type of documents every night, which appeared to be from government departments. He also questioned Sharma about the peon who brought the documents, but Sharma was drunk and hesitant to provide any further information. It was clear that Sharma had some idea about the papers' illegal origin but only cared about making money on the Xerox charges of Re 1 per page.

Ved Prakash felt the daily visits were a burden on Subhash Sharma's pocket and decided to buy his alcohol instead. Every evening, he bought his booze and took an autorickshaw. He and Sharma laughed and joked while waiting for the peon from the nearby office to emerge late in the evening. Unfailingly, the peon would come with his papers late in the evening. It was clear that the peon was copying them on instruction, and Subhash Sharma was doing it for the extra 50 paise that he was earning. Although both were not guilty of any sabotage, they were valuable links that could not be disturbed. Ved Prakash wanted to gather evidence and felt it necessary to steal a paper that the peon would bring. As the machine worked noisily, Ved Prakash picked up a piece of paper and stuffed it in his pocket. That was the first evidence that the network of Coomar Narain yielded in twenty-five years of its existence.

On that evening, Ved Prakash had to attend a wedding of a colleague's family. He did not look at the paper he took from the Xerox shop and stuffed it in his coat pocket. The following morning, he read the paper and realised that it came from the Central Intelligence Bureau. He felt a sense of pride because his hunch was correct. From his Lodhi Colony residence, he went to Bharti Nagar to meet Roy.

Ved Prakash spread the paper in front of Roy and said, 'Your boys said nothing was happening there. But then what is this?' Roy was electrified. He jumped from his seat and ran inside his house. A few minutes later, he emerged with a determined look on his face. Roy alerted his office about the expose. The Intelligence Bureau had failed miserably in the previous few years, which had damaged its reputation. It was supposed to provide crucial information about protecting the state but had failed. The assassination of Indira Gandhi at her official residence had hurt the Intelligence Bureau's reputation even more. The discovery of papers from a Xerox shop was startling information and needed to be investigated.

Roy gathered his handpicked team of men in his office and asked Ved Prakash to discuss the discoveries made so far with them. Ved Prakash suggested that the Xerox shop owner was not involved and should not be disturbed. Instead, they should focus on tracking down all the people who brought the papers to the address where the peon worked. With the tip-off and the discovery of the papers in Coomar Narain's possession, the Intelligence Bureau planned a thorough surveillance operation of the Rohit House Xerox shop. A team of Intelligence Bureau officials were stationed in the surrounding area, and the Aggarwals, the owners of 16 Hailey Road, were informed of a routine law and order recce.

The Intelligence Bureau officials were instructed to wear plain clothes and carry large brown paper envelopes as a way to identify each other. These envelopes were also used to carry walkie-talkies, and some officials were given wireless sets. One person was positioned at the entrance of Rohit House to keep a close watch.

That evening, the script followed its predictable pattern. Sharma and Ved Prakash drank whisky as the peon arrived and quickly made Xerox copies of the papers. 'These are all thieves. They supply these papers to Bombay and big companies. Every day,' said Sharma, counting his money. It was clear that the intelligence briefs sent to the Indian Prime Minister's Office were taken out the following day and sold to corporate houses and other individuals who could pay for them. As soon as the peon left, Ved Prakash walked out and stopped beside him. He pointed out the peon to an Intelligence Bureau person with a large envelope, and the person followed him discreetly. After confirming he came from the SLM Maneklal office at 16 Hailey Road, the Intelligence Bureau officials decided to put twenty-four-hour surveillance around the area.

The Intelligence Bureau field operatives monitored the movements of the peon to his residence in Aliganj over the next few days. They kept a close watch on the comings and goings at 16 Hailey Road from nearby locations. As a result, the entire network of information suppliers for Coomar Narain was exposed in the weeks leading up to the 17 January raids.

During this time, the country was in the midst of an election and there were numerous meetings taking place in the corporate and diplomatic worlds. The Intelligence Bureau operatives were able to pinpoint the names of those involved in these meetings, including P. Gopalan, T.N. Kher, Ashok Jaithka, B.K. Aggarwal, H.N. Chaturvedi and the meetings between Coomar Narain and several of his foreign associates.

9
The Raid

In the early 1980s, Coomar had reached middle age. He had an ailing wife and owned several large properties, operating from the same office on Hailey Road. Despite his personal struggles, he had achieved great professional success and celebrated it with those he considered his trusted friends. Scotch whisky was his steady evening companion. But overall, there was a sense of stagnation as his network had grown significantly but was now facing pressure from a regime that believed in a different way of doing business. Signs of change were all around Coomar Narain, a veteran of the information profession for twenty-five years, who was now suddenly slowing down.

17 January 1985 was an important day. The new government of Rajiv Gandhi was just settling down in his office and Delhi was buzzing in anticipation of the decisions that the young prime minister was expected to take. Coomar Narain, expectedly was curious to know what the new government's policies would be. As expected, His evening plans were disturbed as his special guest that evening delayed his arrival. The informer was his old friend P. Gopalan who worked in the Prime Minister's Office. It was almost 11 pm when Gopalan arrived with a briefcase and finally reached 16 Hailey Road. P. Gopalan had previously been employed at the Home Ministry and worked alongside Kerala Governor P. Ramachandran, who served as the Minister of Energy during the Janata party government. Gopalan had also worked with A.B.A. Ghani Khan Chaudhary

of West Bengal, who had served as Minister for Coal and Mines. Gopalan was attached to P.C. Alexander's office at the time of his arrest.

Coomar opened a bottle of whisky and the two sat down for a round of relaxed chat. They chatted about the day's developments, including the first cabinet meeting held by the Rajiv Gandhi government. The government, with its massive parliamentary majority, was determined to crack down on security to prevent any repeat of recent events. While the two friends were relaxing, they heard a knock on the door.

Coomar and Gopalan were surprised by the intrusion as they were not expecting anyone else. A team from the Intelligence Bureau stormed in and found notes from the cabinet meeting on Coomar's table.[1] The notes were a testament to Coomar's ability, as the meeting had ended barely one and a half hours earlier. The team restrained Coomar and Gopalan and began searching the office. The search lasted until the next morning. At one point, the team found a small consignment of good quality alcohol, including fourteen bottles of Ballentine's finest scotch whisky, six bottles of Black Dog whisky, two bottles of McDowells Diplomat and one bottle of Carew's Blue Riband gin.

On the evening of 17 January, the Aggarwal family had a family dinner and learned only late that night that the police had closed the main gate of their property due to an investigation taking place in the part of the bungalow where Coomar had his office. Before this, the Intelligence Bureau, officials of the Central Bureau of Investigation and the Delhi Police officials held a final meeting to discuss the upcoming raid.[2]

Coomar Narain and P. Gopalan were taken away to the Red Fort for questioning. Police vehicles were also dispatched to the homes of several other officials who had been in contact with Coomar Narain. The first round of arrests was dramatic. The First Information Report filed at Tilak Marg police station on 17 January night named eight persons who had illegally accessed and shared national security documents.

The first batch of arrests included T.N. Kher, a Kashmiri who had previously worked with various high-ranking bureaucrats before becoming the personal secretary to P.C. Alexander in 1980. Alexander was a very influential bureaucrat in the Prime Minister's Office during Indira Gandhi's tenure from 1980 to 1984. As Alexander's private secretary, Kher had access to the entire Prime Minister's Office, including P.N. Dhar, V. Shankar and C.R. Krishnaswamy Rao Sahib. Next was K.K. Malhotra, who was on deputation at the Prime Minister's Office from the Home Ministry.

T.N. Kher, K.K. Malhotra and P. Gopalan were working in the Prime Minister's Office, and their arrests were at the top of the pyramid of the Coomar Narain network. It was the visit of these three officials to 16 Hailey Road that had concretised the allegation of information pilfering brought to light by Ved Prakash Sharma.

The next person in line was S. Shankaran, a senior personal assistant to the President's Press Secretary, Tarlochan Singh. As per a media report, Shankaran had been a part of the president of India's staff for over twenty years and resided in the Presidential Estate. He originally hailed from Madurai, Tamil Nadu.

On the morning of 18 January, Geeta noticed an unusual police presence near her house. While working on the farm, she tried calling her residence in Defence Colony, but no one answered. Sensing that something was wrong, she quickly summoned her driver to take her to Defence Colony. As she entered the house, she felt that something was amiss. She quickly grabbed all the important documents and cash that she knew about before leaving the scene. Geeta rushed back to her farmhouse. The farmhouse had a large backyard and storage area where she could safely keep her possessions without anyone checking. Once the police came to the Defence Colony house, they did not find anything valuable apart from the fact that Coomar Narain and his family lived a luxurious life. Geeta Narain owned the farmhouse in Mehrauli, and her businesses operated from there.

While Geeta was gathering her thoughts, police started interrogating Coomar Narain in the Red Fort interrogation cell. What was surprising was how calm Coomar Narain appeared. It was as though he had arrived at his destination and was prepared to discuss his journey. Coomar Narain spoke candidly about his life as a lobbyist for SLM Maneklal.[3]

After spending his first two weeks in custody, Coomar Narain was moved to Tihar Jail, where he had the company of many terrorists who had been captured from insurgency-affected regions such as Punjab and Kashmir. In addition to that, he also had the company of Rajendra Sethia, who was accused of bank fraud, and Charles Sobhraj. The environment in the jail contributed to his deteriorating mental and physical health, and he fell ill frequently, requiring multiple hospital admissions under police supervision. During his time in prison, his paranoia grew worse. He would stay up at night, waiting for the assassin he was certain would come after him. He also began to disturb the entire ward by howling and screaming.

Despite the efforts of others to convince him that he was imagining things, he continued to insist that someone was trying to kill him. He began discussing the case of Rustom Sohrab Nagarwala, who was part of the infamous Nagarwala scandal. The case allegedly involved the withdrawal of Rs 60 lakhs from the State Bank of India's Parliament Street branch. The case was murky because the bank manager claimed that he had given the money to Nagarwala after receiving a phone call from Prime Minister Indira Gandhi herself. The case caused a sensation in Delhi in 1971, but it could not be properly investigated due to the mysterious death of Nagarwala in police custody. Another police officer involved in the case also died in an 'accident'. Coomar Narain also discussed the case of Sunder Daku, who was drowned in the River Yamuna by a team of Delhi Police officials. It was alleged that Sunder Daku, who was known for his violent crimes, had threatened to kill Sanjay Gandhi, Prime Minister Indira Gandhi's younger son. The incident occurred in the middle of the Emergency in 1975 and shook Delhi with the display of ruthlessness from the official machinery.

Coomar used to claim that he was being framed for the misdeeds of others and that he was not guilty. He feared he, too, would meet the fate of Sunder Daku and Nagarwala inside prison. People like Rajendra Sethia have recollected seeing him weeping endlessly. Such was his condition that within the first two months of his arrest, he lost nearly 20 kg. By April 1985, he weighed around 65 kg. Some supervisors in Tihar Jail even joked with him that the weight loss was good for him and would help him live longer.[4]

After his arrest, Coomar's life took a turn for the worse. Although the investigation and arrest were kept under wraps, the news eventually leaked when G.K. Reddy of

The Hindu broke the story. The news spread rapidly, and Coomar Narain soon became a feared name. Newspapers began to refer to him as the 'kingpin' and 'mastermind'. India was already in a volatile situation stemming from the assassination of Prime Minister Indira Gandhi, the anti-Sikh pogrom, the Bhopal gas tragedy, and the spy scandal only added to already heightened public anger. Coomar Narain was provided high security during court appearances as there were fears that he could be assassinated.

On 4 February 1985, SLM Maneklal suspended Coomar Narain's service. This was a big blow for him. Geeta Narain informed the media that she had received two letters from SLM Maneklal's office in Bombay, which revealed the company was eager to cut ties with Coomar Narain. By then, Coomar Narain had undergone a profound transformation and decided to confess.[5]

Coomar Narain was involved in the business of lobbying, where lobbyists are expected to keep their past deeds and sources confidential. But Coomar Narain decided to break this norm and speak up, which eventually led to the end of his career of the past three and a half decades. It is likely that Coomar Narain realised that he would not be able to avoid imprisonment if he continued to deny any wrongdoing. Thus, he chose to come forward and disclose all the interactions he had had over the past thirty-five years.

The main news of the day was the confession of Coomar Narain, which received more coverage than the return of Tamil Nadu chief minister M.G. Ramachandran from his medical procedure in the US. According to the *Times of India*, Coomar Narain recorded a fifteen-page confessional statement on camera, revealing that at least three countries were involved in the espionage case he was suspected of and that he had been in the business of selling secrets for twenty-five years.[6] Coomar Narain confessed to acquiring and selling government documents to foreign customers in exchange for cash, specifically mentioning the French, Polish and Soviet Union embassies among his clients. He also implicated his employers, the Maneklals, as beneficiaries of his activities.

During the Coomar Narain scandal, one of the names that came up was that of Mrugesh Jaykrishna, a millionaire from Gujarat. Jaykrishna was known for his political influence and had served as the vice president of the Board of Control for Cricket in India and president of the Cricket Control Board of Gujarat in the early 1980s. In 1982, he gained attention when he sold a 50-acre plot of land near Gandhinagar in Ahmedabad at a very low price. He wanted the land to be used for building a stadium in the name of Prime Minister Indira Gandhi. However, several Congress leaders from Gujarat wrote to Mrs Gandhi, warning that the land may become a bigger problem for the Congress party than A.R. Antulay's Indira Gandhi Pratibha Pratishthan case in Maharashtra. It was widely known that the Congress chief minister of Gujarat Madhavsinh Solanki was close to Mrugesh Jaykrishna.[7]

As the media in Delhi pursued the spy scandal, an extensive search was underway to locate the money that Coomar Narain had possibly given to his employer, Yogesh T. Maneklal, and his company, SLM Maneklal. After Narain's revelations, the investigation focus shifted not only to Maneklal but also to anyone closely connected to the group. Similarly to how Ved Prakash Sharma stumbled upon the scandal by chance, a possible link between Mrugesh and the Coomar Narain case arose mainly because of an 'incident'.

On 19 March 1985, two business executives, Chandrakant Amin and Ashutosh Nanavati, who were associated with Mrugesh Jaykrishna, arrived at Sahar International Airport in Bombay. As they approached the immigration counter, Amin noticed that the customs officers were watching him and that his luggage had been marked by some airport officials. This meant that he was a 'circled passenger' and had been selected for a random check. At one point, Amin took out a packet from his suitcase and attempted to pass it to his colleague Nanavati's suitcase, which had not been marked by the customs officials. However, the officials caught this mistake and quickly arrested both of them. It was later revealed that intelligence teams had been tracking the movements of people associated with Jaykrishna, as investigators in the Coomar Narain–SLM Maneklal case had found a connection between Mrugesh Jaykrishna and the Mumbai-based company.

Reports suggested that Amin and Nanavati had had lunch at Bombay's Cricket Club of India (CCI) with Jaykrishna before leaving for the airport that day. When the two were searched, Rs 46.63 lakh worth US dollars in currency and travellers cheques were found on them. The two quickly confessed that they were attempting to take the money out of India and that Jaykrishna had given it to them. Jaykrishna was at the domestic airport at Santacruz and was preparing to board a 7.30 pm flight to Ahmedabad.

The two executives were interrogated, which led to Jaykrishna's own interrogation. Jaykrishna confessed that the foreign currency seized was his own money.[8] Amin and Nanavati told investigators that the money was headed for Hong Kong, and Jaykrishna said that he planned to transfer the money from Hong Kong to his wife's relatives in the United States.[9]

The main issue, however, was why the investigative agencies were so keen on a transparent probe of Mrugesh Jaykrishna. In reality, his rise to success was linked to SLM Maneklal. Jaykrishna's father, Harivallabhdas, was one of the directors of SLM Maneklal and had been one of its key supporters since the company's early days. During the Coomar Narain scandal, Harivallabhdas's connection with the firm raised questions. Jaykrishna was arrested for trying to smuggle out hundreds of thousands of dollars, and investigators were trying to find out where the money came from. Investigators are trying to find out if it was part of the pay-offs for spying.[10] There were obvious hints that part of the money that Coomar Narain had earned through his foreign intelligence contacts in recent months was being siphoned out of the country. One publication asked why a big businessman like Jaykrishna, whose family concerns, including a foreign collaboration project in Thailand, had an annual turnover of Rs 133.33 crore, would need to adopt this method of purchasing illegitimate dollars and sending them through a courier in a hastily planned operation.[11]

Following the discovery of cash and media attention, Jaykrishna was removed from his directorial positions at Gujarat Industrial Investment Corporation and Gujarat Tyres Limited. His wife Parul, who accompanied him to high-profile events, was removed from her position at Gujarat Tourism Corporation. Additionally, the elderly Harivallabhdas resigned from his position as the chairman of the Gujarat State Fertiliser Company. It is unclear how a forty-year-old businessman managed to make such a significant impact on the state of Gujarat and provide land for the Motera Stadium. However, the answer may lie in the political connections between Harivallabhdas and other Congress leaders in the state.

Several news reports alleged that Jaykrishna received 'undue patronage' from Chief Minister Madhavsinh Solanki. During that time, about sixteen textile mills in Gujarat were shut down, but only Jaykrishna's textile mill, Sarangpur-2, received the benefits of the Relief Act.[12] Those who operated within the Coomar Narain–Maneklal network of friends and well-wishers were not anonymous or weak but rather part of the power structure that moved India. They were also a part of the ruling party that governed from New Delhi. The investigation into the Coomar Narain controversy revealed the bigger truth of the Indian political and economic system, and the elements of that truth were highly inconvenient. Interestingly, the prime minister had authorised an investigation that was quickly catching up with members of his political party, indicating that the Gujarat wing of the party was somehow linked to the corporate entity at the centre of the storm.

The news reports on the Coomar Narain case did not contain any information about Ved Prakash, nor did the Intelligence Bureau reveal details of their investigative methods in uncovering this network. There was widespread criticism that such an elaborate network was able to operate within the highest levels of government, and the argument was made that it should have been uncovered much earlier. However, the truth is that if it had not been for the existing association between the Xerox shop owner Subhash Sharma and Ved Prakash, the case would have remained unexposed, and Coomar Narain would have continued operating in a similar manner even during the Rajiv Gandhi years.

One question, however, remains: why did Coomar Narain take a risk by photocopying the papers outside 16 Hailey Road, especially as he could have purchased a photocopier for SLM Maneklal?

Sitting in his Shakarpur residence, Ved Prakash explained that there were bureaucratic restrictions on buying photocopying machines in Delhi at the time. Although businessmen had enough money to buy Xerox machines, they needed a special licence that revealed foreign currency-related information, which could have highlighted Coomar Narain's corporate lobbying and information sale. This was a risky move as India was suffering from foreign currency scarcity, and the government wanted to control every import coming into the country.

To avoid attracting attention from state agencies, Coomar Narain chose to use a Xerox shop near his office. This was usually a cosy arrangement, with the peon paying an extra fifty paise to copy a page. Coomar Narain was a corporate lobbyist and an international operator for over twenty-five years. His career came to an abrupt end in January 1985, but in his lifetime, he probably never knew that Ved Prakash played a significant role in exposing his work. Ved Prakash and Coomar Narain never met each other, and the Intelligence Bureau, which conducted the investigation, kept its sources confidential. It probably also helped the Intelligence Bureau and Roy, as Roy had faced difficulties after his tenure in the Shah Commission, and the Intelligence Bureau itself had failed to provide adequate information to Prime Minister Indira Gandhi in 1976, which led her to end the Emergency rule and call for an election in the spring of 1977.

Ved Prakash played a role in the Coomar Narain investigation of 1985 and beyond. He worked for the Central

Bureau of Investigation and later became the Station House Officer of Delhi Police in Vivek Vihar after 1986. He then served in airport security at Delhi's International Airport before finally being promoted to Additional Commissioner of Police. Throughout his career, he lived in Lodhi Colony and remained focused on his family. He retired in 2002 while serving in the Delhi Police's VIP security wing. Ved Prakash notes that he did not gain any professional benefits from his involvement in the Coomar Narain network discovery. However, J.N. Roy went on to achieve professional success. He received a coveted posting abroad and spent three years in a comfortable position.

The Intelligence Bureau said that it gave Ved Prakash Sharma a financial reward for helping uncover the Coomar Narain network. However, he was unimpressed by the officials' acknowledgement.

'One day, Roy told me that they probably could not give my work greater acknowledgement because there were several powerful foreign countries involved in the Coomar Narain case. They wanted to keep my name a secret,' said Ved Prakash Sharma, arguing that it was probably done to keep him safe. The security situation in the 1980s was tricky and involved Sikh militants and other cross-border threats, and the authorities probably felt it right to avoid major media exposure to Ved Prakash. Yet today, Ved Prakash Sharma suspects that his superiors may have wanted to take credit for the operation, which was publicised as an international plot against India. Regardless of the motivations of his superiors, Ved Prakash Sharma's contribution was crucial to the success of the mission.

In January 1985, the atmosphere in the Indian capital was suffused with conspiracy theories. The election had been fought in the aftermath of a series of major events, such as the assassination of Prime Minister Indira Gandhi and the anti-Sikh pogrom. The Bhopal gas tragedy also occurred between the election and the pogrom. People were unable to make sense of these serious events and, therefore, relied on rumours and gossip. When news of the spy exposure broke and the prime minister made a statement in Parliament, it caused a public uproar. Political parties organised rallies outside the diplomatic missions of various countries in protest against perceived interference in India's internal affairs by foreign powers.

On the day of the first appearance of the suspects from the Coomar Narain network, a large crowd gathered at the Patiala House court premises. The crowd was demanding revenge against the suspects, whom they considered to be traitors. Ensuring security for the suspects became a difficult task, given the situation. Photographers who were present at the venue had already taken the first shots of Coomar Narain before the court proceedings began.

For most of the world, Coomar was the only face that the people saw, and even that face went behind handkerchiefs during the court proceedings. The police were clearly averse to the idea of getting the suspects photographed from the very beginning. The level of secrecy and hype surrounding the case was so intense that the suspects were denied all basic rights during the early days. T.N. Kher informed his legal team on 28 January that he had not been allowed to bathe since his arrest on 17 January.[13]

Due to measures taken to conceal the identity of those involved, the media was unable to obtain visuals of most suspects, and they remained mere names. P.C. Alexander was required to step down from his position and was appointed as India's High Commissioner to London. As the case was discovered to have evolved from corporate espionage to international espionage, involvement or negligence by top officials was not investigated.

After the Mrugesh Jaykrishna episode, the investigation into the larger angles of the case was not pursued, possibly due to fears of political consequences. Despite some investigative teams visiting Paris in search of Alain Bolley, Lt. Col. Alexi Morvan, Otto Wicker, Jan Haberka and Gennady Afanasyvich were not pursued across the world. The collaboration between Alain Bolley and Coomar Narain had emerged as the largest part of the scandal, and it was necessary to investigate the case from the French angle. However, the Indian investigators claimed they were not given the necessary time to explore that angle. The public spectacle of finding the perfect enemy halted abruptly, just as suddenly as it had begun

In the months following the arrests and detentions related to the Coomar Narain spy scandal, the investigation plateaued. This led to a trial that dragged on until 2002, during which Special Judge R.K. Gauba convicted fourteen individuals, including Yogesh T. Maneklal, for violating the Official Secrets Act. One of the first individuals who was arrested, A.P. Sarthi, an employee of the commerce ministry, passed away on 20 September 1986. The court acquitted Ashok Kumar Sharma and B.K. Aggarwal, while Ashok Jaithka was discharged in 1985. Several people, such as Coomar Narain and T.N. Kher, received bail after a few years of imprisonment

Coomar Narain passed away on 20 March 2000 before the case was closed. Those who were convicted in the case included Yogesh T. Maneklal and P. Gopalan, who was present with Coomar when the Intelligence Bureau officials came to arrest him, C.L. Chanana, Swami Nath Ram, K.K. Malhotra, S. Shankaran, Amrik Lal, Jagdish Chander Arora, V.K. Palaniswamy, Jagdish Tiwari, H.N. Chaturvedi, Kishan Chand Sharma and T.N. Kher. The SLM Maneklal group was also convicted. In July 2002, Yogesh T. Maneklal received the maximum sentence of fourteen years, and ten others received ten years of rigorous imprisonment. On 8 March 2010, the *Times of India* reported the news of Yogesh T. Maneklal's death. With Yogesh's passing, the last of the prime characters of the Coomar Narain spy scandal left the scene.

10

Two Secrets

Edwin Walder arrived at New Delhi Railway Station on a winter evening in 2019, having taken the Rajdhani Express from Mangalore. It had been more than half a century since his last visit to the city. Delhi was crowded and the air was difficult to breathe.

The city had changed dramatically since he last saw it. The crowds and the noise made him feel disoriented, and the memories he had of the city were lost in the haze of time. Although he was no longer the handsome young man he once was, he still had strong arms and a heavy neck. As he made his way through the crowd on the railway platform, carrying a small bag, he remembered the day his grandmother received a letter from his mother in Delhi. For years, Edwin had been upset that his mother, Gerty Walder, had left him in Mangalore and gone to Delhi. In the innocence of his childhood, he believed that his grandmother's love was the same as maternal affection. However, one day, Gerty called him from Delhi, and his comfortable world in Mangalore was disrupted as he was uprooted to be united with a mother who was a stranger to him.

In the all-male line-up of the Coomar Narain network, Geeta Narain's presence was never considered during the investigation into espionage. The investigation failed to focus on understanding the personal, political and international circumstances that could lead to even a common man chasing his private dreams to provide strategically important information detrimental to his country. However, the story of Coomar Narain would be incomplete without the story of Geeta Narain and her bold venture into Delhi from Mangalore as a single woman with a heart full of secrets.

Geeta and Coomar, two humans with aliases, had built a prosperous existence for themselves in the Indian capital. They had important friends in political circles, earned a great deal of money and spent it in style by buying properties in the happening places of the capital and planning for the future. But in the midst of all this, there was a gaping vacuum that was filled with personal failures in building a family and the inability to belong to those who were indeed their family. To better understand why Coomar Narain may have acted without caution in the changing scenario of Delhi, his empty domestic scenario should be taken into consideration. The couple built properties, but they appeared increasingly lonely in these properties.

Two souls uprooted from their homes due to circumstances found themselves in the new capital of the new India. They came together and formed a perfect team – Geeta looked after their home and properties and businesses, while Coomar was a busy corporate lobbyist. However, their choice to take on aliases in their new lives indicated a lack of acceptance, and they were always considered outsiders despite their prosperity.

When the spy scandal broke, Geeta Narain was contacted by the media. She tried to portray her relationship with Coomar Narain as broken. '…we did not get along very well. He has his own life and I am happy with the farm and my work here,' she said to journalists Vinod Sharma and G.K. Singh, who wrote perhaps the only news report of the spy scandal that had valuable observations on Geeta Narain.[1]

However, her argument is contradicted by the reality of their lives. Geeta Narain was the one who handled most of the money and property-related matters in Coomar Narain's private life, and she was the one who called the shots. In 1973, she wrote a letter to the authorities stating that she was selling her Nizamuddin residence to the 'Bharat Sewa Trust' of Allahabad, a trust run by the influential Sherwani family of Uttar Pradesh.[2]

Coomar Narain was successful in navigating the Indian capital, but his wife was just as capable at home, making it a true partnership. Were the Narains the Rosenbergs of India? Were they ideologically motivated? Did Coomar Narain's superiors in the government service treat him disrespectfully, which might have made him amoral and even antithetical to the Indian state?

The motivations behind Coomar Narain's actions were both financial and personal. There is no indication that his actions were motivated by ideology or hatred towards the government or the state. Instead, he appears to have been a deeply alienated person who relied on his strong-willed wife, who complemented him well. He was polygamous in professional relationships, and according to media reports, he may have also been polygamous in his personal life. However, it seemed he trusted only Geeta with his safety and secrets. As someone who left behind only his actions and not voluminous diaries, his motives can be understood through the personal and professional decisions he made. There is no evidence of ideology playing a role in his choices.

While he shared information with the Soviets, he had the longest collaboration with Poland, which had a complicated relationship with the Soviet Union. But in the end, the French benefitted most from his work. There are indications that Poland also benefited from Coomar's papers, but this has not been conclusively proved. Nonetheless, the names of several Polish diplomats continue to be linked with the Coomar

Narain scandal. The fact that he went overboard while helping the French showed that Coomar Narain was willing to go all out for the Western European players. Perhaps they paid better, or maybe he simply liked them more.

It was clear that Coomar was an amoral business broker who prioritised profits over nationalism and security. But the palpable tension at home with his ambitious wife also played a role that cannot be dismissed.

Shiv Dev investigated the lives of Geeta and Coomar Narain and came across the mention of Geeta in Coomar's confession. 'My wife Geeta belongs to Mangalore', he had said soon after arrest.[3] Shiv Dev travelled to Mangalore and visited the churches of the city. Here, he discovered the truth that Geeta had been trying to run away from. Reports revealed that Geeta was close to a politician and had friendships that had gone sour. More than Coomar Narain, it was Geeta's complicated relationship with her grown-up son Edwin that showed deep emotional conflicts and unhappiness within the Narain household. Geeta did not have sympathy for Edwin, who was likely a part of her past that she wanted to leave behind.[4]

From her temporary residences in Kashmiri Gate, Geeta moved in with Coomar Narain after they got married. Coomar Narain had joined SLM Maneklal in 1960 and they suddenly found themselves in the neighbourhood of poets and artists like Gaitonde and Sanyal in Nizamuddin. Both Geeta and Coomar kept quiet about her past as part of the adjustments they had to make in a distant land away from home. The only time the couple wanted to revisit her past as 'Bibiana Gerty Walder' was when she brought young Edwin to Delhi, overwhelmed by her maternal instinct. But it ended in a small scandal that nearly ruined Coomar Narain's career. Edwin ended up stealing an expensive Fiat from the vicinity of the upmarket 16 Hailey Road, which was the address from where Coomar Narain ran the office of SLM Makeklal.

In 1964, soon after SLM Maneklal had a big breakthrough with Poland, the family was looking forward to brighter days. Geeta thought of trying once sincerely to establish her ties with Edwin. Coomar Narain was successfully established in Delhi and the Narains had established themselves financially. It was 1965 and Edwin was a young man.

Coomar was magnanimous in accepting Edwin as his son. But Edwin was a wild child like his mother. There were loud, emotional clashes between mother and son, and peace vanished temporarily from the Narains' home in Nizamuddin. Edwin began spending more time outside and hanging out with boys who spent their time on the streets. He did not speak the local language, but he connected with them through action.

Geeta trusted her instinct and thought Edwin would be happy with the luxurious life she could provide him. However, that did not happen. Edwin found a rather unique and painful way to protest against it. It was probably his way of punishing his mother for leaving him alone with his maternal grandmother, Juliana.

Every day, Edwin would pace up and down the distance between the main gate of 16 Hailey Road and the house in the back, where music, poetry and drama could be heard. This nearby building served as a hostel for the graduate students of the National School of Drama. Coomar was a medium-built man who appeared stocky in the winters due to the woollens he wore. The residents of 16 Hailey Road would watch this man with a determined expression who would rarely interact with others. They would do that with caution and silence. He was a mystery of sorts for the children of the house and the neighbourhood, who played on the grassy lawns of the mansion. Sometimes, the children would see grown-up men with briefcases come and go from Coomar Narain's office. It was an undisturbed small world, which would soon be disrupted by Edwin.

Coomar Narain would drive the boy to his office, and the young boy would spend some time in the front yard of 16 Hailey Road with other children from the neighbourhood. Coomar Narain introduced Edwin as his son, which he indeed was in principle. On a good day, the father and son duo would come to the office of SLM Maneklal. Although Edwin could barely speak Hindi, communication was the least of the problems.

Edwin was a tall young man, a little over twenty years of age. His rippling muscles spoke of youthful energy. He was at an age when young men thought of creating a future for themselves. However, Edwin did not have that opportunity. He tried to fit in with the boys of his age but could not get along with the boys of Nizamuddin's aristocratic homes. He had no natural talent for music or the arts, and the only thing he was good at – sports – was not appreciated by his parents, who expected him to pick up the skills of the smart offspring of the usual government residences. Nonetheless, Edwin secretly learned how to drive. He befriended the garage owner behind the 16 Hailey Road mansion and would go on drives with his newly found friends. Edwin soon demanded a car from his parents.

Neither Geeta nor Coomar Narain was ready for this expensive demand and did not want to give in. A month after his birthday, Edwin had a big fight with Geeta one morning. He then left in his stepfather's car and arrived at 16 Hailey Road, where he proceeded to the yard. There, he saw a new Fiat car in the front yard. The Aggarwal family, who owned the house, had been considering buying a new car for months. However, buying a car was not an easy task then and required a lot of effort. The family had applied for the car and had waited for several months, with frequent checks with the dealer in Connaught Place. Finally, on that day, the car was driven home in the morning.

The glistening machine caught Edwin's eye, and he became obsessed with it. Soon after discovering the machine, he stopped fighting with his stepfather and mother and instead focused on getting ready on time to accompany Coomar. Every day, after reaching his office on Hailey Road, he would rush out to the driver's garage in the backyard, where he would discuss how to obtain a driver's licence. Unknown to Coomar Narain and Geeta, Edwin had been secretly working towards acquiring a driver's licence. He kept this a secret by paying a little extra to the garage owner's son. Before long, he had obtained the coveted driver's licence.

With the licence in hand and improved driving skills, Edwin returned to playing with the children once again. In the morning he would play with the children, followed by work in the office until evening. After that, he would take a nap on the couch in the office and then engage in sports with the children near the car parked in front of the house. No one had noticed Edwin's fascination with the car and that he had managed to locate the car keys.

One day, after a particularly late round of hide and seek, Edwin asked Coomar for permission to leave, which was granted. He left the mansion's courtyard unnoticed. Coomar Narain and the mansion's owners did not even hear the sound of the Fiat as it hummed outside on a chilly winter evening. Coomar Narain left in his own car, followed by his staff. None of them noticed that the brand-new Fiat was missing from the front parking area.

Coomar Narain reached his house in Nizamuddin and discovered Edwin had not yet reached home. Thinking of it as one of the teenager's usual tantrums, the Narains retired for the night, hoping the boy would eat his dinner kept on the table. But Edwin did not return. Morning came, but Edwin's food was still on the table. The Narains were seriously worried.[5]

Residents of 16 Hailey Road were alarmed when they discovered that their car was missing from the shed. Further investigation revealed that the car key was also missing from the tray. Despite their efforts, they were unable to find any leads. Coomar Narain arrived for work that morning to find that the police had been called to register a case of a missing car. However, he did not reveal that his son had also gone missing on the same day as the car. The Narains remained silent and considered their options. However, they did not have to wait long as Edwin drove the car all the way to his grandmother's house in Mangalore, where the police were able to track him down and recover the car.

The police team drove Edwin to Delhi, with him seated between two police officers in the backseat. This was an embarrassment for the Narain family, as Edwin had ended up at the Tilak Marg police station due to committing an auto theft. It was unclear why Coomar Narain's adopted son had committed this crime and what his motivations were. These questions remained unanswered. However, it was clear that the past and present do not always match seamlessly. Interestingly, the family at 16 Hailey Road mansion had forgotten about the case until they were reminded of it during a meeting with the author about the old tale of 1965 when an expensive car was stolen from the porch and the culprit was found to be the son of the tenant Coomar Narain.

Coomar Narain was deeply hurt by Edwin's act, but it was worse for Geeta, who felt betrayed. There are no records of what transpired between the son and the mother, but it can be assumed that Geeta suspected that her son was deeply disturbed by her absence from his early years and had decided to hurt and tarnish her reputation in Delhi as revenge against her. It was Edwin's revenge against his mother, who had abandoned him as a child and had now returned to reclaim him after attaining everything in life.

The scandal was the last straw that broke Geeta and blocked her from reconnecting with the past that she wanted to own. The mother in her never healed. Geeta sent Edwin back, and they never saw each other again. Some years later, Edwin married and had a son named Prakash who knew of his grandmother but never met her. Edwin told the boy that his grandmother had passed away.

Edwin had to come to Delhi in 2019 because he was facing trouble at home. News had spread that his long-lost mother had left him a very large fortune in Delhi, which came as a surprise to Edwin's family as he had never mentioned her before. The news of the fortune brought unwanted attention to Edwin from curious strangers and real estate agents. In a moment of desperation, Edwin thought of seeking help from the only sympathetic person he had met in recent years – Sub Inspector Shiv Dev Singh Dahiya of the Delhi Police.

Months earlier, Shiv Dev had arrived in Mangalore to investigate the case of the property that the Delhi Police wanted to hand over to the rightful heirs. Edwin's meeting with Shiv Dev helped solve the case. It was revealed that Coomar Narain and his wife Geeta Narain indeed had an heir who could rightfully inherit their property in Delhi. Edwin became a local celebrity overnight. The sudden transformation and attention from people made him uneasy and disturbed him deeply. Edwin, who had lived a life as a former petty criminal and small-time automobile repairman, found it difficult to understand the chaos that had surrounded him. The situation pushed him to the brink of insanity, and he left his home on the Rajdhani Express to seek security and solitude in Delhi.

When Shiv Dev arrived at his office, he found Edwin waiting for him at the reception of the Delhi Police headquarters. As he listened to Edwin's account of events and watched his disoriented state, Shiv Dev felt sad for him. He decided to host Edwin for a couple of days and assured him of his safety. After some convincing, Shiv Dev managed to persuade Edwin to return to his home in Mangalore, assuring him that he could come to Delhi to claim his inheritance when the courts gave the final order. Edwin eventually realised that the news was not fake and that he did indeed stand to inherit his mother's property. Although the case has been dragging on, Edwin continues to remain in Mangalore while he waits to inherit his mother's property.

From the time Shiv Dev was tasked by his superiors in the Economic Offences Wing of Delhi Police with uncovering information about Coomar Narain's property, three different angles emerged – Narain's property, his personal life and his infamy, which made him a person of interest. At first, Shiv Dev was only interested in Narain's property, but over time, he discovered details about his personal life and chunks of his espionage scandal. The links varied and often crisscrossed the entire lifespan of Coomar and Geeta, which exhausted Shiv Dev. He could not initially understand how the Narains had a son in Mangalore and not in Delhi. His investigation, like any story on Coomar Narain, faced the strong barrier of silence as anyone who knew Coomar Narain refused to speak or even acknowledge that they knew him.

Shiv Dev was disturbed by Coomar Narain's lonely end. He wanted to find out if any part of the Narain family had cut ties with the controversial man after the espionage scandal was exposed. This was the only way to dispose of the Narain property and prevent it from being taken over by property sharks.

With this in mind, Shiv Dev searched through the case files of Coomar Narain kept in the Ambedkar Nagar and Tilak Marg thanas, where the few remaining papers on the lives of Coomar and Geeta Narain are still kept. While searching through the documents, he found an old Pongal greeting card sent to Coomar Narain and his family by a famous masala maker based in Chennai. The card was among the documents recovered from Coomar's residences in Defence Colony and office at 16 Hailey Road. It was a eureka moment for Shiv Dev as it indicated that Coomar had surviving relatives in other parts of India. However, the question remained whether they would acknowledge their ties with a man convicted of espionage.

Shiv Dev flew to Chennai to meet the prominent spice-making family. However, as expected, the family refused to acknowledge any association with a man who was considered a villain in his lifetime. After his persistent efforts, Shiv Dev was finally able to establish that Coomar Narain had a significant number of relatives who were leading successful lives. However, they made it clear that they did not want to be involved in the unfortunate life of their family member who had left for Delhi seven decades ago.

Geeta and Coomar wanted to start a new life in Delhi, hoping to become a respectable couple in the city. However, the arrival of the police at their residence in Nizamuddin due to the car theft scandal was too much for the couple to handle. They decided to move to Defence Colony, and Coomar Narain purchased a large house, C-385. The three-storey building stands out among the modern constructions in Defence Colony, with pink and white tiles on the exterior. Some tiles look like they might fall off at any moment, but despite its decay, the building tells the story of its former glory days.

The Narains' domestic happiness was short-lived as Coomar Narain's desire for a normal family life coincided with his quest for pleasure that his money could buy. Coomar Narain used to entertain his political links that he rarely saw later on. One of his political connections ultimately purchased the Defence Colony property, leaving a lasting imprint that Coomar Narain was politically influential and sought after. In 1983, Congress Member of Parliament Tapeshwar Singh of Bihar bought the property from Coomar Narain for Rs 30 lakh,[6] an enormous sum for the time. This transaction proved the political reach and success that Coomar Narain had achieved by then in the corridors of power.

When the family moved to the Mehrauli farm,[7] Coomar Narain managed to keep a part of the Defence Colony house for himself, where he continued his evening entertainment. In the 1970s, he brought two adopted kids to the Defence Colony residence. After the Coomar Narain spy scandal erupted in the world news, Radha (also known as Radhika) fled from the luxury farmhouse in South Delhi to reside in Nangloi. Radhika now lives in a small residence in a congested part of Nangloi and feels deeply hurt whenever someone reminds her of the past. Finding Radhika was not easy. It was Geeta Narain who informed the media that she had two adopted daughters, but they both vanished soon after Coomar Narain's arrest on 17 January 1985. To track Radhika, one had to go through old media reports and Delhi Police records where she was mentioned. Radhika claims that Geeta and Coomar had major differences, and the mother would often hit the two adopted girls. Coomar Narain had to intervene to protect them. Another account suggests that Radhika and Renuka were two maids employed by the couple, along with others. Regardless of the versions available, it appears that the two girls were much younger than the others employed at home.

Some people say that when the Narains' luck ran out, their daughters abandoned them as well. It was well-known that the Narains did not have any biological children. However, the discovery of Radhika through police files revealed that Coomar and Geeta Narain's personal life had fallen apart mainly because they did not agree on how they wanted to live. They maintained cordial ties and Coomar Narain trusted Geeta completely, but they also gave each other space. Geeta ruled over the farmhouse, while Coomar Narain led an independent life in his office and the spare rooms of the Defence Colony address. The two had tried to create a semblance of normalcy by bandaging the unevenness and the dysfunctionality of their lives. Finally, they failed to hold both the personal and the professional fronts.

Decades have passed since the make-believe heaven of normalcy created by Coomar Narain's business practice and complicated domestic life crumbled. However, the locals who worked in his farmhouse continued with their lives like muted sparks from an exploded munition. The

Narains have long gone, but they are still remembered in alcoholic outbursts in police stations and the villages on the outskirts of Delhi. Policemen who interacted with them recall them as cordial and gentle people who had mysterious foreign friends.[8]

Geeta and Coomar purchased several large properties in Delhi over a span of three decades, but none of them, except one, bears their name. The only property that still bears Coomar Narain's name on the wall is where the couple spent their last years. According to police sources, they lived a solitary life in the large house, taking care of each other with the help of three servants. Money was never a problem for the Narains, even after Coomar Narain stopped working due to the scandal. The Narains tried to protect each other just as they did in their younger days in the 1960s. Occasionally they welcomed strangers into their home, and one such stranger was a local car salesman named Ajay. The couple treated Ajay as their own, and he was impressed by their humble behaviour. Coomar and Geeta's reputations did not reflect in their behaviour towards others.

Ajay became part of Coomar Narain's household. Geeta's small poultry and dairy business provided them with a meagre living, but they had a large collection of art at home, which was a testament to Coomar Narain's power and influence in Delhi. In 2000, the Coomar Narain case had been going on for about fifteen years. Coomar Narain was vilified by the media as a deadly spy. It was at this time that he had a fatal heart attack. It was a swift death after Coomar collapsed at home with his wife beside him. Ajay was called immediately. Unfortunately, there was no way to revive him. Despite the many pressures he faced over the years, Coomar Narain remained steadfast in his career until his heart finally gave out. Ajay found it very difficult to cope with the situation personally.

With Coomar Narains's death, the long-winded case lost its star. The occasional court hearing that used to draw the media contingent to the court premises lost appeal. Geeta lived without a purpose and meaning. The crisis that had returned her husband to her had altered her life forever. He had drifted away from her when he acquired the millions and returned to her when he had lost the battle against the Indian elite, who safeguarded their own from harm but were happy to sacrifice the outsider Coomar Narain.

According to Ajay, the couple were simply two lonely individuals trying to cope with their age. Without Coomar, Geeta spent her days wandering around her property in casual attire and rarely went out in public.[9] Gone were the days of beauty parlours and perfumed evenings. The only person who saw her were the young local businessman Ajay and the three domestic assistants. The local police occasionally checked on her to make sure she was doing well. There were rumours circulating about the mysterious woman and her collection of antique jewellery.

Geeta had reportedly promised to leave her property to the people who looked after her during the last days of her life. However, before that formality could take place, a stranger walked into her house and the dogs saw him. Though there were no witnesses to the crime, the dogs' fear-filled eyes spoke volumes. Geeta Narain was found murdered on 7 December 2002, a few months after the Coomar Narain case had ended in the summer of that year.

Like Coomar, there was no shortage of flowers for Geeta, who loved flowers and fragrance. Two individuals who aimed for perfection and prosperity in life were laid to rest by complete strangers. When Geeta Narain died, she was a character on the margins and she captured the media's attention only once, when press photographers captured her standing outside the Mehrauli farmhouse of Coomar Narain.

The story of the mysterious Narains did not come to an end with Geeta Narain's cremation. Several unanswered questions remained about Coomar Narain's alleged espionage and doubts persisted. The most intriguing aspect of the Coomar Narain scandal was that the case was entirely based on the official version and the media reports of the time rarely questioned the overwhelming accusations thrown at Coomar Narain.

The story of Coomar Narain was narrated forcefully by the powers that wanted only one version to survive, which held Coomar Narain guilty in the public's perception. The state's eagerness to accuse Coomar raises questions about what the Coomar Narain spy scandal was all about. Were Coomar and his network of stenographers and secretaries working together for decades? Or were there more important and better-connected people who were perhaps not investigated?

As far as accessing Indian defence secrets was concerned, it is widely known that Coomar Narain was not the first or the last person to access them. The issue that caused outrage was not the access to these secrets but the fact that they were accessed by those outside of the circle of power, such as stenographers and clerks, who are typically considered inferior to their superiors Additionally, the fact that these individuals were able to benefit financially from this access caused the systematic quake. This can be explained by the fact that there was no substantial examination of the foreign angle beyond the expression of displeasure through diplomatic channels to France, Poland, East Germany, Soviet Union. However, Coomar Narain himself had confessed that he had been active in the field of information for close to twenty-five years and that he had evidently been rather amoral in acquiring and sharing information among his clients in Delhi's diplomatic circle.

The spy scandal involving Coomar Narain has lasted for a long time, partly because Coomar himself never talked about his exploits to the media. However, Roger Faligot, Jean Guisnel and Rémi Kauffer have now reported that there was indeed an intelligence operation to access Indian defence secrets. The objective of this operation was to make French defence items more attractive in a market where Moscow had a long-established monopoly. So, it is safe to say that Coomar Narain was a participant in Operation Nicobar, run by the French. There are likely to be similar plots related to other countries that, unfortunately, may never come to light because no investigation was conducted on them. Nevertheless, the Coomar Narain spy scandal stands out because it shows that the elite are not always in control of the narrative. There are times when those who exist without agency of their own can play a role in shaping the course of the state. A proper investigation would have unearthed far more uncomfortable truths, as has been indicated in the previous pages. However, in the absence of that, it is Coomar Narain who has to bear the cross alone.

Afterword

For nearly four decades, the Coomar Narain spy scandal has been hanging like an incomplete painting on the walls of the history house of India. The spy story had exploded on the front pages of newspapers, causing an unprecedented public frenzy at a time when India was looking for a perfect enemy to blame for the traumatic moments in its national history. The story of a business lobbyist who sold the country's secrets in exchange for money was the perfect narrative for the nation that was grieving in the aftermath of the assassination of Indira Gandhi and a series of violent incidents that had left India traumatised. The story came up with lots of questions but not all of them were answered satisfactorily. To create a perfect enemy, the portrait of Coomar Narain had to be ready. But that never happened. The scandal left many unanswered questions. The perfect enemy that India was looking for never materialised. In these pages, the reader may find that Coomar Narain was far from being perfect. He was indeed an imperfect man with his own share of problems and insecurities.

On 25 June 1975, Prime Minister Indira Gandhi imposed the Emergency rule which resulted in unprecedented censorship on the media. However, surprisingly, this led to a boom in the media industry. Several news magazines were launched in Delhi, Kolkata and Bombay. In 1976, television also acquired its own space with the birth of Doordarshan and the separation of TV from All India Radio. News began an exciting journey. From that time onwards, Indian media did not look back as the young first-generation post-1947 professionals took charge of the newsroom. The media scene changed with a mix of new and old magazines and fortnightlies like *Fortnight*, *Surya*, *India Today*, *Sarita*, *Vanitha*, *Sunday*, *The Week*, *Blitz*, *Illustrated Weekly* and *Dharmayug*. Intrigues and spy stories were a staple of these publications.

Spy scandals and news about spying were not new in the Indian media. There was a man named MAK,[1] an East African diplomat. While Alain Bolley and other customers of Coomar Narain's network received information in exchange for Black Label bottles and sex, MAK was the one who stored all the wine and supplied money. The source of his seemingly unending finances became clear when one day, in a state of drunkenness, he boasted to fellow diplomats that his 'analytical reports' to the United States Embassy led to the removal of an American from a sensitive department to a less important one in the embassy in Delhi's diplomatic quarters. What kind of East African diplomat would send 'analytical reports' to the US embassy in the Indian capital!

During the early 1980s, MAK used to visit Hyderabad and Bombay frequently, spending several days there. These visits were so important that he even missed the birth of his child in a South Delhi clinic. Unfortunately, this was also a time of communal violence in both Bombay and Hyderabad. MAK had become so well entrenched in the capital's discussion groups that he had become a member of the 'Thursday Club', consisting of prominent Indian writers, politicians, bureaucrats and foreign affairs experts.

There was much more information to be uncovered, but it could only be achieved if the searches and raids were conducted in complete secrecy. Unfortunately, the news of the operation spread across the Indian capital, which led the new prime minister to inform Parliament about the spy network that had been unearthed.

MAK and Bolley were part of a large network of defence attaches and politically inclined diplomats who took advantage of Delhi's 'non-aligned' environment and implemented the worldview that was spread with conviction by Marie Murat in DGSE.

Looking back in time, the modality of stealing papers from the Prime Minister's Office appears like an uncertain and risky method. Surveillance and espionage have evolved significantly over the years, surpassing what was once thought of as science fiction in the early 1980s. But given the sensitivities and stature of the office of the Indian prime minister, stealing documents from the Prime Minister's Office was not an unsophisticated operation either. It required continuous monitoring of sources and officials like S. Shankaran, T.N. Kher and P. Gopalan – all of whom were among the first to be arrested during the evening when Coomar Narain was picked up from his office in Hailey Road. Nurturing sources in the highest offices of India required a certain kind of skill and agility that was not in the domain of Bolley. That expertise belonged to Coomar Narain, the local anti-hero. The terms that the team members shared could not be disturbed at any point and they had to be maintained in crucial locations throughout. The ground-level soldiers of Operation Nicobar, consisting of Indian personnel of Coomar's group, were no less sophisticated when viewed from the perspective of the final delivery of their work. The sophistication required was not of technology as the actual operation required the French to rely more on human intelligence or HUMINT and less on TECHINT. Operation Nicobar, therefore, was specifically devised for a low-tech developing economy with significant economic potential.

The question, however, is whether the French were the only ones involved in high-end economic espionage. The answer is no. The Soviets were also involved in similar activities. However, the Soviet plot did not display the kind of bold vision that the leaders of SDECE had shown in the 1970s when they saw an opening opportunity for their fighter aircraft in India. The Soviets were already an established force and did not show the same level of aggression that the French brought to the craft. Nevertheless, they, too, engaged in economic espionage targeting the defence deals.

Surrounded by a green belt, Jawaharlal Nehru University, located on the edges of the city, gained fame by the early 1980s as a centre of scholarship and revolutionary ideals. Its lecture halls resounded with the debates of students and teachers, and its canteens hosted PhD students almost daily as they celebrated successful defence of dissertation on the India–Soviet relationship, economic models and political theory. In addition to its academic excellence, the university had a feisty political reputation.

The university was located at the far end of the city and was rather isolated from the busy life of the city. It was in this setting that a stunning Russian student met Daljit Singh Thakur, a handsome Air Force clerk who walked into the campus to get a degree in the language.

The School of Languages of Jawaharlal Nehru University had become a hub for some of the finest scholars in languages as diverse as German, Russian, French and Persian – each one important academically and also carrying strategic importance. The government encouraged defence and foreign service employees to learn a foreign language. Daljit Singh Thakur, an intelligent young man in his early thirties, decided to learn Russian as it could help him and increase his chances of travelling abroad or making friends among the visiting Russian delegations as they often did as part of the India–Soviet defence partnership. Before he could spot any visiting Russian delegation selling spare parts for the MiGs, Thakur spotted Rita. As they bonded over their common love for the language, people started to talk about the Indian boy winning over a Russian beauty. The terms between Daljit and the Russian lady did not betray anything sinister as it appeared more like a close friendship between two adults.

There was only one problem. The resident KGB representatives in the Embassy of the USSR kept an eye on all Russians residing or transiting through India. Daljit's Russian partner was of particular interest because she was a student. As the vanguard of the communist struggle, students were important to the USSR and being a Russian, she was of even more interest to the resident KGB representative in Delhi.

It is not known exactly how Daljit became acquainted with one of the top KGB officials in Delhi. However, he most probably met the KGB operative on the harmless anniversary of the Russian Revolution celebrations. The anniversary of the Russian Revolution was an important event and was celebrated with gusto in the embassy of the USSR. It was most likely there that he met Nikolay Golobov[2], the Soviet official.

By 1984, the Soviets had a growing basket of troubles in South Asia. The Afghan Mujahideen, with support from General Zia of Pakistan, posed a formidable challenge to the Soviet forces. India was no longer the close ally that it was in the early 1970s. The year 1984 began as the election year, and there was a growing feeling in the air that Indira

Gandhi, who had a turbulent four years, would call for an election before the end of her tenure. It was during this time that newspapers announced the upcoming visit of Marshal Dmitry Ustinov, the powerful defence minister of the Soviet Union, to India.

It was a weeklong visit and marked a new level of dialogue between India and the Soviet Union that began in 1982 after the death of the elderly Soviet leader Leonid Brezhnev. Brezhnev's death was the end of an era for India and Indira Gandhi, as the Soviet leader was a key supporter of India–Soviet friendship.

After a transitional phase under Andropov, a new ruler took charge in Moscow in February 1984 with the arrival of Konstantin Chernenko. India–Soviet relations were highlighted by the Indian side, with newspapers announcing the visit on 4 March. The visit's atmosphere had to be carefully protected, but all did not go as planned. Towards the end of the visit, the script went wrong.

On 12 March, Prannath Lekhi, Supreme Court lawyer and a staunch anti-communist activist, sent a telegram[3] to the Minister of Home Affairs, P.V. Narasimha Rao. In the telegram, he revealed that the Indian government had arrested and expelled a senior Soviet spy named Nikolay Golobov. Golobov was caught accepting classified documents from a lower division clerk from the Air Force headquarters. The following day, Golobov was forced to leave for Moscow. In view of the upcoming visit of the Soviet defence minister, the Indian government wanted to suppress the news of the arrest and expulsion. However, the irrepressible Lekhi leaked the news to the media three days before Ustinov's arrival in Delhi.

It was at this time that on 6 April, Daljit Singh Thakur had a visitor in his R.K. Puram office in the southernmost part of Delhi.[4] The visitor was firm. He wanted to see Mr Thakur's identity card. Once he received it, he examined it and placed it in his pocket and promptly served Mr Thakur with a dismissal order. The order was signed by a senior official known for cracking down on corruption cases. Thakur was taken away and interrogated extensively. He was first interrogated in a dark park on Tughlaq Road and then in the deserted tombs in Lodhi Garden at night.

After a few sessions of sustained interrogation, Thakur signed a confession stating that he had met a Russian girl named Rita at Jawaharlal Nehru University, where she was a student in the Russian language course. How Thakur met Rita was not important. What was important was that Rita introduced Thakur to someone in the Soviet embassy who became his friend. The three of them would often drive to Badkal Lake outside the capital. The Soviet official wanted to know what the French, Iraqi and Nigerian visitors to the Indian Air Force facilities were looking for. He asked many questions, usually over vodka and whisky, where Rita was just a mere presence. The Russian diplomat often limited his interaction to Thakur.

Thakur spoke freely to his interrogators as he felt he had nothing to hide. As a result, he was not prosecuted. Consequently, he was not charged because his interaction with Soviet diplomat Nikolay Golobov did not reveal any criminal intentions. He just did not care for anything beyond the good time with Rita and the lakeside get-together in Badkal Lake. The diplomat was none other than Nikolay Golobov.

However, one outcome of these interrogations was that the Indian government was now certain that the Soviets had a far-reaching espionage network that targeted high-level officials in India. Golobov was only one part of the network. The Soviets used the Coomar Narain network in a more indirect way, relying on proxies to gather information.

The Daljit Singh case, which occurred just before the Comar Narain spy scandal broke out, revealed the extent of foreign intelligence operations in the Indian capital and helped in piecing together the motivation behind the intelligence networks that intersected in Delhi under the shadow of various corporate and diplomatic players.

Investigators found that Coomar Narain was sharing strategically important information with the Soviets through his special sources and business friends. However, it was unclear why the Soviets, despite being a friendly country, would be interested in spying on the office of the prime minister. The Soviets were nervous about protecting their turf and preventing poachers. This move was not a confident one by a superpower on the rise. While the Soviet use of Coomar Narain demonstrated a deep understanding of the Indian system, it was no match for the French in terms of vision and boldness.

The Coomar Narain case revealed that Moscow was becoming increasingly jittery about the arrival of competitors to India. The investigation into Daljit Singh Thakur's case showed that KGB Major Nikolay Golobov was on the lookout for 'advanced technology coming in from the West'. The Soviets were already well-established in India, and an advance alert from Coomar Narain obviously helped them deter their rivals better.

The main actors in the Soviet ring were not located in Delhi but in Ludhiana, which had become the centre for textile and woollen products. Out of this city came two businessmen who dealt in hosiery. Ashok Jaithka and B.K. Aggarwal were attempting to secure export orders to Eastern Bloc countries like the USSR, Poland, East Germany, among others. Indian traders exported nearly Rs 3,000 crores worth of goods annually to the Soviet Union and to gain a share of this mammoth market, they had to befriend an insider in the commerce ministry. The two businessmen befriended a person named H.N. Chaturvedi, an assistant at the textile department of the commerce ministry. On one of their trips to Delhi, the three of them went out drinking to a bar in nearby Connaught Place. After a few drinks, Chaturvedi started boasting and said they should try to obtain some 'real information' instead of just information about the government's export plans. He claimed to know someone who was supplying real information, referring to his friend Coomar Narain, who had invited him to occasional parties and information-sharing trips to the office of SLM Maneklal on Hailey Road.

Jaithka and Aggarwal worked as a team and were in contact with the trade representatives of the Soviet embassy in Delhi. However, they were not aware that the trade representatives of the Soviet embassy were actually professional intelligence officials. Soon, the 'trade representatives began instructing Jaithka and Aggarwal on the type of information they should demand from Chaturvedi. As a result, Jaithka and Aggarwal were able to obtain military information from Chaturvedi. The irony and the blackmail involved in the situation were evident. Jaithka and Aggarwal wanted export orders from the Soviet Union, but the trade representatives would only help if they received solid information about the activities of R&AW and the Sino-India relationship.

However, the Soviet Union's interest in India was not hostile, but they were determined to gather detailed information about India's key sectors. Specifically, they desired military documents detailing troop movements. This was because India's troop movements, particularly with regard to Pakistan in the western and northwest sectors, would allow the Soviets to assess the pressure that General Zia was facing from the Indian government under Indira Gandhi. If India concentrated a large number of troops on the western border, General Zia of Pakistan would automatically bring his troops from the western border with Afghanistan, where the Pakistanis were aiding the anti-Soviet Afghan Mujahideen fighters.

The Soviets rewarded Jaithka and Aggarwal handsomely for this work. Aggarwal had earned Rs 18 crore in the previous few years, while Jaithka, a new entrant, received export orders worth Rs 2 crores.

The Coomar Narain case unfolded in stages. On the first night of the raid, it seemed that only the French were involved. However, it was later discovered that other countries, including the Soviets, Poles and East Germans, were also involved. However, the French were found to have conducted the most sophisticated operation. Coomar Narain spoke of his French contacts first, as the officials dealt with him directly. But after a few days he revealed the name of H.N. Chaturvedi, who was also arrested. Chaturvedi then revealed the names of two Ludhiana businessmen and the demands they made for military documents. The Intelligence Bureau reached Ludhiana and arrested Jaithka from his residence. He surrendered after spending two hours in the toilet.

The more experienced Aggarwal sensed trouble as soon as he heard about Coomar Narain's arrest. He had enough money to live comfortably abroad and even owned a house in Delhi, where he stayed during his trips to the city. He quickly packed his bags and took a flight from Palam Airport to Bombay. However, the Intelligence Bureau was already present at Sahar Airport and prevented him from boarding any other flights. They put him on a flight to Delhi, where he was arrested on board.

The exposure of the Golobov–Daljit Singh Thakur axis led to the full circle of the Soviet part of the espionage ring. The arrest of Coomar Narain and Ashok Jaithka–B.K. Aggarwal duo was a part of it.

The network of Soviet agents who were in touch with Daljit Singh Thakur and the more elaborate network of agents of Moscow that was expelled after the arrest of Coomar Narain showed the Soviets wanted to stay on top of the race. Papers related to India's negotiations with both the West and the USSR for the MiG-25, Foxtrot Reconnaissance Squadron, three Kachin class destroyers and the security apparatus of the Prime Minister's Office were found in Coomar Narain's possession. While exposing the Coomar Narain's network was a crucial step, the revelation of the Soviet network's extent, which had been operating since the early 1950s and continued uninterrupted till the 1980s, demonstrated how deeply Moscow had penetrated the Indian state through its ground network in the capital.

During the Nehruvian and the Indira Gandhi years, several intelligence operations targeted India, including the placement of a nuclear-powered device in Nanda Devi aimed at spying on neighbouring China. However, the Coomar Narain scandal was of a different degree. Rajiv Gandhi had emerged victorious in the December 1984 election and the media was full of writings about how the prime minister planned to transform the country. The old order within the political elite was facing challenges from within and crumbling, while new thinking was taking hold in the corridors of power. It was at this time, a fortnight after the election of the new government, that the spy scandal surfaced. This was a moment of catharsis for modern India. The Larkins brothers scandal also emerged at the same time, but it did not receive the same degree of vilification and media trial as the Coomar Narain scandal. The Larkins brothers came from the known sections of the bureaucratic and military elite of India. It involved Anglo-Indian brothers, Major General Frank Larkins and Air Vice Marshal Kenneth Larkins. The Larkins brothers were accused of passing Indian military secrets to the United States and Fabrique National of Belgium. In contrast, the Coomar Narain scandal was far more dramatic. The Larkins brothers were regulars at the Delhi Golf Club. The Coomar Narain case was a significant event for the Indian people and TV viewers because it marked the first time that an Indian spy was brought into the public eye.

However, unlike the heroic portrayal of spies in movies, Coomar Narain was not a hero. The media portrayed him as a villain, but it is unclear whether he was actually a villain or a victim of a society that found it convenient to create a story that suited their needs.

A fortnight after the spy scandal broke out, the famous Dravidian politician M.G. Ramachandran returned to India from the United States, where he had undergone a kidney transplant and medical treatment after suffering a stroke. MGR, as he was famously known, had been away for most of the previous months when major events like the assassination of Indira Gandhi and the election of December 1984 that brought Rajiv Gandhi to power took place. His return from New York was expected to be a massive public event. Two lakh people stayed overnight in the Mohite Stadium of Madras to greet MGR as his flight landed at the Madras Airport. MGR received a tremendous public welcome. However, the next day's the *Times of India* did not find that spectacular public event in Chennai worthy of a lead story. Instead, the main headline of the *Times of India* on 5 February 1985 was about the Coomar Narain scandal – 'Coomar Narain Makes Confession: France, Poland, GDR named behind network'. The public interest in the 'biggest spy scandal of India' was enormous, especially given that Indira Gandhi had been assassinated just four months earlier, and there was an air of suspicion and paranoia across the country. Coomar Narain's activities suited the prevailing mood of India that the Larkins brothers could not match.

The scandal that he took government documents and passed them to European powers like France has been corroborated by French investigative journalists. What made Coomar stand out in the entire saga was that, unlike the Larkins Brothers, he was a complete outsider who had climbed his way up, and no one had noticed anything unusual about his activity in the corridors of power. The fact that someone with connections to government stenographers could penetrate the system sent a message throughout the bureaucracy about its poor surveillance capability. The Coomar Narain scandal thus marks the beginning of surveillance governance in post-1947 India, which would become more creative as government agencies perfected techniques for tracking both government officials and common people.

The spy scandal instilled fear of official secrets in the Indian bureaucracy. After the fortnight of the scandal surfacing, a climate of fear prevailed in the top offices of the Government of India in New Delhi. The *Times of India* reported on 22 January 1985 that the Intelligence Bureau had started scrutinising the biodata of all officials working in the North and South Blocks, which housed the Ministry of Home, Ministry of External Affairs, Ministry of Defence and the Prime Minister's Office. In addition, the Union home minister S.B. Chavan announced in Parliament that government agencies would scrutinise all those linked to the Coomar Narain network. The bureaucracy had never experienced such a fear factor, which would leave a permanent impression on the way papers moved across the corridors of power in the Government of India offices in the capital. The scandal also put an end to the way lower sections of the political class functioned. Until then, the second- and third-rung leaders had their own importance, but after the scandal revealed that a number of second- and third-tier leaders were involved with the network, it triggered a centralisation of political authority in the ruling Congress party, which was followed by the BJP subsequently. The scandal marked a clear departure from the past of Licence Permit Raj when ferreting official information for profit was part of the norm. Less than a decade later, liberalisation was announced, and many of the things that were necessary for lobbyists to survive in India were no longer necessary. More sophisticated lobbyists were required with more sophisticated tools for the trade that Coomar was known for.

The Coomar Narain scandal was significant for India as it was the first time the country had seen a spy. 'A spy does not enter the government service. A government servant is enticed to become a spy,' a counter-intelligence chief of India wrote this in a file in the 1970s to argue for periodic review of the security clearance of government officials.[5] By that definition, the Coomar Narain scandal highlighted not just one collector of intelligence but several people who were collecting intelligence. He was focused on getting official secrets to help a foreign government secure a big defence deal with India. At the height of the scandal in 1985, the public was so frenzied that there were fears someone in the crowd attending the court hearings daily would shoot

Coomar Narain and kill him. Coomar Narain was seen as a villain, the enemy of the people.

The story of Coomar Narain made headlines during my childhood. Though it appeared on TV and even in the international media, it was mainly a print media story that recorded every twist and turn of the story in detail. Unfortunately, the reporting failed to lift the story beyond the ring of espionage. The story remained in print for the next one and half decades as I moved from Kumarghat to Delhi via Chennai, referred to as Madras in those days. While names of cities and streets have changed with time, Coomar Narain's story is a link with India's past in which business, politics and espionage were conducted differently and power was exercised differently too. The story of Coomar Narain, therefore, is worthy of exclusive treatment. The big question is, was Coomar Narain a spy, a corporate lobbyist or both? Or was he an outsider who failed to get away with something that another resourceful person would have managed to play successfully?

It was reported that Coomar Narain made a confession that was video recorded. However, the story does not end there. Coomar Narain subsequently denied his confession, though it did not make much of a difference as he was expected to be convicted due to the official stance on the case. Coomar Narain passed away in 2000 before the long-drawn court proceeding came to an end in 2002. Indian sources did not provide evidence of Coomar's wrongdoing or the involvement of Yogesh T. Maneklal in the scandal that led to the downfall of SLM Maneklal. On the other hand, French investigative journalists Roger Faligot, Jean Guisnel and Rémi Kauffer provided a version of the scandal that implicated French intelligence chief Pierre Marion and Alain Bolley. According to their accounts, Coomar assisted the French in obtaining defence procurement secrets from the Ministry of Defence and the Prime Minister's Office, which helped Paris win one of the largest defence contracts that India had approved in the first four decades of its independence.

By his own initial admission, Coomar had been active in similar activities for twenty-five years. Although it cannot be confirmed if he helped foreign agents in the 1960s, it appears he crossed the line of official secrets by collaborating with French officials in Delhi. It is unclear how much information Coomar shared with his foreign contacts and employer, and the details may never be known. It is uncertain if Coomar was motivated by ideology or financial gain or if he found himself in a situation beyond his control. Despite the Cold War–era ideology, Coomar likely was not ideologically driven. The Coomar Narain scandal was a public frenzy that allowed the investigation to drift away and not explore many angles, such as the psychological aspects of Coomar's personality. His wife Geeta Narain was a private person who did not want to revisit her past. Coomar's unhappy personal life may have influenced his choices. While fluid identity is useful in intelligence, Coomar was not an underground operator but instead worked by befriending those he felt were available in a ferocious city. India stopped looking for the enemy once it became clear that finding the real enemy would be embarrassing.

At the end of the day, it cannot be claimed that *A Singular Spy* will answer all the questions related to the Coomar Narain spy scandal, but it is an attempt to provide a complete picture and give honest answers to some of the lingering questions about the lead characters of the case – Coomar Narain, SLM Maneklal, Geeta Narain and the French, Polish and Russian figures as well as the inconvenient links to the establishment. Hopefully, this will help complete the incomplete portrait that has hung on the walls of India's history house for so long.

Author's Note

Writing about a heroic life is relatively easy as many people step up to share their experiences on the subject. However, writing about a character who was vilified in the media and condemned widely in society poses a particularly difficult challenge for a researcher. Researching on Coomar Narain was one such affair where people who knew him perhaps felt hesitant to share information about him. That, however, did not prevent the less privileged ones, like his foster daughter Radhika, from coming forward. When I tracked her down in Nangloi, on the outskirts of Delhi, Radhika clearly remembered many of the incidents, including her memory of living on Geeta Farms, where she and her sister Renuka were brought at a very young age to work. They felt at ease on the farm and believed that Coomar Narain was a great support to them. However, their peaceful phase ended abruptly when he was arrested. She vividly recalled that Geeta hastily emptied the cabinets that were overflowing with whisky bottles and dumped some of them in the backyard to prevent the police from discovering them during their raids.

A lot of research could not have been possible without Sub Inspector Shiv Dev Singh Dahiya of the Delhi Police. He took over the case of the property of Coomar Narain, which resurfaced in 2008 and collected documents on the subject. The story of Coomar Narain had ended, but Shiv Dev brought it back to life. The documents he collected shed new light on Coomar Narain and his personality and helped this book enormously.

Over the years, several individuals have assisted me in reconstructing the lives of Coomar Narain and Geetanjali. I am grateful to former Tihar Jail superintendent Subhash Sharma, former Chief Press Officer of Tihar Jail Sunil Gupta, Delhi Police SI Surinder Kumar and SHO of Kalkaji police station Sandeep Ghei for their generous assistance. Despite initial reluctance, they eventually agreed to meet with me and shared details that they felt would aid the narrative. I am also thankful to Rahul Rawat of Jawaharlal Nehru University, who provided a solution to the research bottleneck that I was facing and was very generous with his help.

The Coomar Narain story was a challenging one to work on due to the harsh treatment that Coomar received from the media from the outset. He was referred to as the 'kingpin' of the spy network. Reports in leading newspapers and magazines were filled with salacious gossip about his multiple female friends and alcohol-fuelled parties. Additionally, both Coomar and Geeta had used various names throughout their lives, which made it difficult to determine the correct name to use. For the sake of convenience, I have decided to stick to the names 'Coomar Narain' and 'Geeta' or 'Geetanjali Narain', as those were the names used in the first media reports that surfaced in January 1985.

Based on the early reports, the spy scandal seems to have resulted from an internal conflict within government agencies. There were obvious power struggles between the Intelligence Bureau and other law enforcement agencies, and as a result, certain agencies were brought to the forefront while others were not highlighted.

Many of those reports were well-researched and presented honestly by the reporters and editors who wrote them. However, these did not tell the whole story of the Coomar Narain scandal. Although the scandal was uncovered in Delhi, Coomar Narain had worked for the Bombay-based firm SLM Maneklal throughout his corporate career. The story that spread across the country was created in Delhi and left out the interesting role of SLM Maneklal in the previous decades when the company grew to become one of the most important engineering firms in the country. The company was highly respected, and it is unclear how it got involved in a murky story of intelligence and technology exchange in the high streets of statecraft. Another question that needed to be explored was how a lobbyist who had worked quietly for a quarter of a century became a spy working for foreign governments. These were just two of the major research questions that needed to be answered. However, the main challenge in researching the Coomar Narain story was that people generally avoid talking about those whom the mainstream media portrays as villains. To make matters worse, Coomar did not give interviews after his release from Tihar jail in the mid-1980s on bail and passed away quietly before his conviction.

However, the media again came to the rescue to tell the full story of Coomar Narain. Like many other frenzied media coverages, the Coomar Narain scandal was recorded extensively. However, in the frenzy of the moment, it was not highlighted that Coomar Narain's employers were not unknown small-time businessmen but rather tall figures who often found space in newspaper columns.

During my research on Coomar Narain, I found great research resources in the old archives of *The Times of India* Mumbai edition, which regularly reported on the industrial career of SLM Maneklal and its parent company, T. Maneklal. The fascinating archives of the newspaper held the story of how a school dropout maverick Gujarati businessman, Trikamlal Maneklal Chamdawalla, started the company against the backdrop of the Second World War and the anti-colonial struggle. Afterwards, advertisements, news and advertorials – advertisements that were packaged to look like news – were published in *The Times of India*. *The Times of India* digital archive that I used to reconstruct the lifespan of SLM Mankelal gives an idea of how widespread the coverage of this company was in its time. It is likely that many more archives on this company remain in old private media collections. However, much of it is lost forever as it was not digitally preserved.

This sea of advertisements, news and analysis, as well as the employment opportunities announced by SLM Maneklal, played a crucial role in rebuilding what this company was like in its lifetime from 1941 to 1985. The story that emerged was not just of Coomar Narain but rather a story of India's industrial journey and the evolution of a post-colonial society. This society had to deal with challenges posed by the sharing of technology, which many public and private sector companies continue to face today. The Coomar Narain spy scandal was not just the story of a villainous lobbyist selling government files to French, Polish, Soviet and US representatives. It was also a story of India's industrial class that grew in the post-1947 period with political support, often struggling to overcome crises.

The media coverage of the Coomar Narain spy scandal was Delhi-centric. However, to fully understand the story, it is important to also consider SLM Maneklal from Mumbai and the European part. I have provided a detailed analysis of the corporate history of SLM Maneklal and the French plans, in order to cover all three segments of the story.

Newspapers are often considered the first source of historical documentation. However, in the case of SLM Maneklal, archival research has shown that they can also serve as a repository of information that can be brought to light decades later. In 1985, some claims were made regarding SLM Maneklal's international collaborations that were presented in a twisted manner. But newspaper records from Mumbai revealed that most of these claims were based on decades of technology transfer under the Government of India's regulations. Each of these partnerships was proudly advertised in Mumbai's newspapers and the success of the company's collaborations, such as with shipping major Centromor of Poland and plastic moulding collaboration with Toshiba, were documented in newspaper columns and advertisements. However, it is another matter that the government later turned on the company after the Coomar Narain scandal came to light.

These documents, to some extent, corroborate the widely reported 'confession' of Coomar Narain that his work required him to stay in touch with foreign embassies and companies that were interested in accessing the Indian market. While there were obviously other Indian business houses that also required technology exchange, the story of SLM Maneklal stands out as it conducted technology exchange with both power blocs of the Cold War era, ultimately leading to its downfall. Apart from my personal collection of Coomar Narain-related media reports, archival materials from *The Times of India* were invaluable in establishing the historical space occupied by both Coomar Narain and his employer, who during its better days was among the best-publicised engineering companies in the country.

Research on Coomar Narain was not an easy task. However, I received immense support from Red Ink Literary Agency, which stood by me during the last few years as the work progressed slowly. It was only during the pandemic that I started writing the story, as the world around me was in crisis. The unexpected interest shown by a film production house in the story helped me focus on the work. I express my deep gratitude to Anuj Bahri, whose support helped this project to take flight.

This work is dedicated to my Didibhai Keya Bhattacharya Korantak and brother-in-law Shripad Korantak, who are very special to me. My parents Amita Chakraborty and Keshab Kanti Bhattacharjee – Mamoni and Babu – are partly responsible for my lifelong fascination with the Coomar Narain case. Back in my childhood, the story of Coomar Narain reached us through the magazines and newspapers that my Babu brought home from his favourite newspaper vendor in Agartala and Calcutta's Chowringhee. So this work is also a tribute to Mamoni and Babu's love for news and the lively discussion that continues in our house.

Notes

CHAPTER 1: THE BATTLEFIELD

1 ‘When salt duty is abolished: Middleman’s profit to be reduced’, *Times of India*, 20 September 1946, p.3.
2 ‘Abolition of salt tax: Reported decision of interim government’, *Times of India*, 17 October 1946, p. 9.
3 ‘Middleman in trade’, *Times of India*, 16 March 1911, p. 8.
4 Ibid.
5 Ibid.
6 ‘More crime in Delhi: Economic factors – Constant watch on revolutionaries’, *Times of India*, 18 July 1932, p. 3.
7 Ibid.
8 ‘Ghee scandal case: Official examined’, *Times of India*, 7 September 1953, p. 9.
9 Ibid.
10 ‘Handling of gur scandal case: Defence by three union ministers’, *Times of India*, 5 March 1964, p. 5.
11 Ibid.
12 ‘Govt has lost moral authority to rule, says Dwivedi. Lok Sabha begins debate on No Trust Motion’, *Times of India*,16 March 1965, p. 9.

CHAPTER 2: THE KING OF ALIASES AND HIS QUEEN

1 Mahender Singh Manral, ‘Coomar Narain: A spy and how his stepson came out of the cold’, *Indian Express*, 15 September 2019, https://indianexpress.com/article/india/spy-and-the-son-coomar-narain-spy-case-5995924/
2 Author’s interview with Shiv Dev Singh, Sub Inspector of Delhi Police.
3 Author’s interview with Pandit N.K. Sharma, astrologer of Prime Minister P.V. Narasimha Rao.
4 Long Roll IAPS Centre & Records, from Delhi Police records on Coomar Narain’s personal life.

5 Ibid.
6 Author's interview with Sunil Gupta, former press officer of Tihar Jail. Gupta served during the time Coomar Narain was imprisoned in Tihar during the 1980s.
7 M.O. Mathai, *Reminiscences of the Nehru Age*, New Delhi: Vikas Publishing, 1978.
8 The impression about Coomar Narain's communication skills is based on the interview that the author conducted with Radhika, Rajendra Sethia and jail superintendents of that time.
9 'Subhadra Joshi to head Delhi PCC', *Times of India*, 21 April 1978, p. 19.
10 The author is thankful to Prof. Sydney Ribeiro, John Dayal and Michael Dias for clarifying this point.
11 Thanks to the rigorous archival investigation by the Economic Offences Wing of Delhi Police, it was established that 'G.N. Mangalore' alias Geetanjali Narayan alias B.G. Walder was the legal owner of the property.
12 Dilip Bobb, Shekhar Gupta and Raju Santhanam, 'Espionage: The spy sensation', *India Today*, 15 February 1985, p. 23.

CHAPTER 3: SIGNS OF THE ENEMY

1 Weldon Bruce Dayton, Appellant, v. John Foster Dulles, Secretary of State, Appellee, 254 F.2d 71 (D.C. Cir. 1958), https://law.justia.com/cases/federal/appellate-courts/F2/254/71/196491/
2 On 28 April 1956, an agreement between India and Canada for the establishment of an atomic research and experimental reactor in Trombay by the Government of Canada under the Colombo Plan was signed at New Delhi. From MEA, *Annual Report, 1956–57*, New Delhi: MEA. p. 37.
3 Ministry of External Affairs, *Annual Report, 1956–57*, New Delhi: MEA. p. 37.
4 'Large-scale espionage in India reported: Increase in activities by Pakistan agents', *Times of India*, 21 July 1949, p. 1.
5 Ibid.
6 'High court admits bail application: Accused in Delhi spy case', *Times of India*, 27 October 1956, p. 9.
7 'Nehru–Dulles talks last over three hours: Reducing Indo-US Differences', *Times of India*, 10 March 1956, p. 1.

8 'Espionage ring in Delhi: Documents seized', *Times of India*, 30 December 1960, p. 1.
9 'I.A.F. spy gets 14 years' R.I.', *Times of India*, 15 December 1963, p. 1.
10 'Death sentence for murder of Arab diplomat', *Times of India*, 27 February 1970, p. 7.
11 'New Turn in Delhi murder case: Many theories on murder mystery', *Times of India*, 4 September 1978, p. 1.
12 'New Turn in Delhi murder case: Many theories on murder mystery', *Times of India*, 4 September 1978, p. 1.

CHAPTER 4: THE COMPANY

1 'Yagnik, leader of mass movement', *Times of India*, 18 July 1972, p. 11.
2 V. Gangadhar, 'Gujarat student campaign fades: Bickering breaks out', *Times of India*, 25 June 1974, p. 4.
3 'Fascists regrouping for final battle', *Times of India*, 1 December 1975, p. 9.
4 'S.L.M. Maneklal cuts dividend', *Times of India*, 11 July 1974.
5 'T. Maneklal: The years of challenge', *Times of India*, 27 March 1971, p. 7.
6 Ibid.
7 Ibid.
8 Ibid.
9 'Prospectus: T. Maneklal Manufacturing Company Limited', *Times of India*, 4 September 1958.
10 Ibid.
11 Ibid.
12 Ibid.
13 Ibid.
14 'New venture by T. Maneklal', *Times of India*, 8 December 1961.
15 'S.L.M. Maneklal to start output', *Times of India*, 7 November 1963, p. 4.
16 Ibid.
17 'Display Ad 11', *Times of India*, 25 December 1972, p. 7.
18 'Notice for Maneklal Scientific Research Foundation', *Times of India*, 7 May 1971, p. 17.
19 Ibid.
20 'New ventures by T. Maneklal', *Times of India*, 19 January 1971, p. 4.

21 'Rexroth Maneklal Industries', *Times of India*, 17 April 1976, p. 6.
22 Ibid.
23 Ibid.
24 K. Balakrishnan, 'Jyoti Limited: An Example of Successful Entrepreneurship', *Case Studies in the Acquisition of Technology (II)*, New York: UNIDO, 1984.
25 World Bank, *India: Survey of the Textile Machinery Industry (With a note on the Indian Cotton Textile Industry)*, New York: World Bank, 1975, p.24.
26 K. Balakrishnan, 'Jyoti Limited: An Example of Successful Entrepreneurship', *Case Studies in the Acquisition of Technology (II)*, New York: UNIDO, 1984.
27 Ibid.
28 Raju Santhanam, 'Spy scandal: Investigating officials get airtight case against arrested people', *India Today*, 31 March 1985, https://www.indiatoday.inF/magazine/cover-story/story/19850215-involvement-of-coomar-narain-in-spy-drama-received-with-shocked-surprise-769798-2013-11-25
29 Vinod Sharma and G.K. Singh, 'Selling the nation's secrets', *The Week*, 3–9 February 1985, p. 20.
30 'Complete plants for the production of Nylon and Acrylic Fibres from Unitechna', *Times of India*, 3 August 1970, p. 3.
31 'Coomar's links being probed', *Times of India*, 28 January 1985, p. 1.
32 Raju Santhanam, 'Spy scandal: Investigating officials get airtight case against arrested people', *India Today*, 31 March 1985.

CHAPTER 5: TEMPLES, SHIPS AND MILITARY SECRETS

1 'Liaison men to be screened', *Times of India*, 23 January 1985, p.1.
2 Vinod Sharma and G. K. Singh, 'Naming the network', *The Week*, 28 April–4 May 1985, p. 36.
3 Ibid.
4 'Defence and nuclear secrets may be out', *The Times of India*, 21 January 1985, p. 1.
5 Vinod Sharma and G. K. Singh, 'Naming the network', *The Week*, 28 April–4 May 1985, p. 37.
6 Ashok Row Kavi, 'Though Profits Declined', *The Week*, 17–23 February 1985, p. 35.

7 Ibid.
8 Ibid.
9 Ibid.
10 An article in *Los Angeles Times*, 4 February 1985, claimed that apart from France, Coomar sold official papers also to a 'second western nation' which it did not name. This report and similar others hint that the Central Intelligence Agency was directly involved in supporting Coomar. It was also guessed that some countries also worked as fronts for the Central Intelligence Agency as the intelligence agency did not want to be involved directly because of the delicate nature of the India–US relationship.
11 Ibid.
12 https://archive.org/stream/dli.bengal.10689.12610/10689.12610_djvu.txt
13 Annual Foreign Affairs Record, Ministry of External Affairs, 1955, p. 209–210.
14 Ibid.
15 'Display ad', *Times of India*, 18 December 1970, p. 13.
16 Ibid.
17 Ibid.
18 'Display ad 12', *Times of India*, 13 November 1972.
19 'City notes: Excellent show by T. Maneklal', *Times of India*, 17 October 1970, p. 4.
20 'Display ad 2', *Times of India*, 25 April 1973, p. 7.
21 'Classified ad', *Times of India*, Bombay, 5 August 1972, p 11.
22 Vinod Sharma and G.K. Singh, 'Was Maneklal the kingpin', *The Week*, 17–23 February 1985, p. 33.
23 Vinod Sharma and G.K. Singh, 'Naming the network', *The Week*, 28 April–4 May 1985, p. 36.

CHAPTER 6: NICOBAR

1 https://apnews.com/article/1f569c99aa5f58e7172030ff91c8c896
2 Roger Faligot, Jean Guisnel and Rémi Kauffer, 'The DGSE and the services in the Indian subcontinent: A long history', in *Histoire politque des services secrets français*, Paris: La Découverte, 2013, 133.
3 Ibid., p. 493. Pierre Marion changed the name of SDECE (Service De Documentation Extérieure Et De Contre-espionage)

4 Roger Faligot, Jean Guisnel and Rémi Kauffer, 'The world without the USSR', in *Histoire politique des services secrets français*, Paris: La Découverte, p.443.
5 Ibid.
6 Rémi Kauffer, *Les Femmes De L'Ombre*, Paris: Perrin, 2019. The term used regarding the attitude of Marie Murat is *d'autodéfensefeminine*, which can be translated to 'a feminine form of defence' or a 'feminine defensive mechanism'.
7 Roger Faligot, Jean Guisnel and Rémi Kauffer, 'The world without the USSR', in *Histoire politique des services secrets français*, Paris: La Découverte, 2013, p. 443
8 Vinod Sharma and G.K. Singh, 'Naming the network: How Coomar Narain and Co went about their job', *The Week*, 28 April–4 May 1985. p. 37.
9 'Suresh T. Maneklal dead', *Times of India*, 16 July 1977, p. 6.
10 Ibid.
11 Ibid.
12 Ibid.
13 Roger Faligot, Jean Guisnel and Rémi Kauffer, 'La IV République et le: SDECE socialiste Ribière, Boursicot et Fourcaud: Les trios figures tutélaires du "SDECE socialiste"', in *Histoire politique des services secrets français*, Paris: La Découverte, 2013, p.84.
14 Ibid., p.494.
15 Ibid.
16 Ibid., p.495
17 Pupul Jayakar, *Indira Gandhi: A Biography*, New Delhi: Penguin, 1992, p. 289.
18 Ibid. p. 494.
19 Murali N. Krishnaswamy, 'Rajiv Gandhi was "entrepreneur" for Swedish jet, US cable says', *The Hindu*, 8 April 2013.
20 Roger Faligot, Jean Guisnel and Rémi Kauffer, *Histoire politique des services secrets français*, Paris: La Découverte, 2013.

CHAPTER 7: A CHARISMATIC FRENCHMAN

1 Vinod Sharma and G. K. Singh, 'Selling the nation's secrets', *The Week*, 3–9 February 1985, p.22.
2 Roger Faligot, Jean Guisnel and Rémi Kauffer, *Histoire politique des services secrets français*, Paris: La Découverte, 2013, p. 494.
3 Ibid., 493.

4 Shekhar Gupta, 'The most complicated character in the Indian spy scandal', *India Today*, 15 February 1985.
5 Author's interview with former CBI official Ved Prakash Sharma, who broke the news of Coomar Narain's network to the Intelligence Bureau.
6 Ramesh Chandran, 'Rajiv Gandhi's visit to Paris likely to put derailed Indo-French ties back on track', *India Today*, 31 March 1985.
7 'India says France is recalling its envoy', *New York Times*, 2 February 1985, https://www.nytimes.com/1985/02/02/world/around-the-world-india-says-france-is-recalling-its-envoy.html.
8 https://www.liberation.fr/grand-angle/2005/11/04/la-chute-de-l-ambassadeur_537838.

CHAPTER 8: NEMESIS

1 Author's interview with Ved Prakash Sharma.
2 Abhinav Garg, 'Year after conviction, HC acquits ex-army officer', *Times of India*, 16 May 2009, p. 14; Lt. Col. S.J. Chaudhary was acquitted more than two and half decades in 2009 by the Delhi High Court which observed the evidence regarding the typescript to be insufficient

CHAPTER 9: THE RAID

1 'Deputy secretary among 4 held in spy case', *Times of India*, 21 January 1985.
2 Vinod Sharma, 'Spies in the PM's office: P.C. Alexander accepts moral responsibility and resigns', *The Week*, 27 January–5 February, p. 23.
3 'Coomar to receive medical treatment', *Times of India*, 17 September 1985, p. 6.
4 Author's interview with Sunil Gupta, former chief press officer of Tihar Jail who was one of the few officers allowed to interact with Coomar Narain. Interview conducted in Delhi on 8 December 2023.
5 'Coomar Narain makes confession: France, Poland and GDR named behind network', *Times of India*, 5 February 1985.
6 Ibid.
7 'Playing foul', *The Week*, 14–20 April 1985, p 11.

8 Kusum Chopra and G.K. Singh, 'Another spy connection: Mrugesh had links with SLM Maneklal', *The Week*, 14–20 April 1985, p. 10–11.
9 Ibid.
10 Ibid.
11 Ibid.
12 Ibid.
13 Vinod Sharma, 'The unwinding secrets: Investigators of the spy case score a small success by eliciting confessions in court', *The Week*, 10–16 February 1985, p. 14.

CHAPTER 10: TWO SECRETS

1 Vinod Sharma and G.K. Singh, 'Selling the nation's secrets', *The Week*, 3–9 February, p. 22.
2 'Sale permission for my building No C33A, Nizamuddin, East, New Delhi', letter from G. N. Mangalore to the Land and Development Officer, Ministry of Works and Housing, Government of India, Nirman Bhavan, Maulana Azad Road, New Delhi 24.
3 Author's interview with Shiv Dev Singh.
4 Gilbert D'Souza's name appears in the documents in possession of the Economic Offences Wing of Delhi Police.
5 There are two versions of events related to Edwin's long drive. According to documents from Delhi Police, the car's owners were alerted about the direction the car was being driven by a garage owner in Aurangabad, who had briefly hosted Edwin during the drive. However, there is another version that disputes this claim.
6 Based on the author's interview with Vinod Kumar, Manager of Biscomaun Guest House, C-385, Defence Colony.
7 'U.S., French and FRG missions involved: Dy. secretary among 4 held in spy case', *Times of India*, 22 January 1985, p. 1.
8 Author's interview with SI Surender of Mehrauli police station. Surender had heard about the wealth of the Narains and shared some gossip from the neighbourhood.
9 This section is based on the author's interaction with a source who was witness to the last years of Geetanjali and Coomar Narain in Sainik Farms in South Delhi. He spoke over the phone,

refusing to appear in person. The author is grateful to Delhi Police for facilitating this interaction. Respecting the wishes of the source, his identity has been left anonymous.

AFTERWORD

1 Vinod Sharma and G. K. Singh, 'The man called MAK: Quite a few embassy officials are not what their designations mean', *The Week*, 3–9 February 1985, p. 23–25.

2 http://insidethecoldwar.org/sites/default/files/documents/Department%20of%20State%20Report%20on%20Expulsion%20of%20Soviet%20Officials%20Worldwide%201986%20January%201987.pdf

3 Ibid., p.5.

4 Vinod Sharma and G. K. Singh, 'Traders and traitors', *The Week*, 3–9 March 1985, p. 3.

5 Vinod Sharma and G. K. Singh, 'Selling the nation's secrets', *The Week*, 3–9 February, p. 18.

Index

About the Author

Kallol Bhattacherjee has been a journalist for two decades, primarily focusing on foreign affairs. He has worked with various leading organisations, such as the Iranian News Agency and *The Week*. Currently, he serves as a Senior Assistant Editor with *The Hindu*. He can be reached at janusmyth@gmail.com.